How
the Church of England
Works

by

PAUL A. WELSBY

CIO PUBLISHING
Church House, Dean's Yard, London SW1P 3NZ

500 899457

ISBN 0 7151 3707 7

Published September 1985 for the General Synod of the Church of England by CIO Publishing.

By the same author:

Lancelot Andrewes, 1555 - 1626
The Bond of Church and State
How the Church of England Works
George Abbot: The Unwanted Archbishop
Sermons and Society
A History of the Church of England, 1945 - 1980

Printed in England by Edward Mortimer Ltd., Halifax and London.

Contents

		Page
Acknowledgements		v
I	The Establishing of the Church of England	1
II	The Province	5
III	The Diocese	7
IV	The Parochial System	15
V	The Parish: The Incumbent	21
VI	The Parish: The Parishioners	27
VII	The Parish: Councils and Officers	31
VIII	The Cathedral	37
IX	The Non-Parochial Ministry	42
X	Church and State	45
XI	Synodical Government	50
XII	The Boards and Councils of the General Synod	57
XIII	The Church's Revenue and Expenditure	63
XIV	The Church's Legal System	68
XV	The Anglican Communion and the Ecumenical Movement	75
Index		82

Acknowledgements

I have used a considerable amount of material, appropriately updated, which originally appeared in my *How the Church of England Works* published in 1960 by SPCK and for many years out of print. I wish to thank the Bishop of Rochester (Dr David Say), the Rev. M. W. Bucks (Staff Chaplain to the Chaplain of the Fleet), Mr Robin Catford (the Prime Minister's Secretary for Appointments), the Rev. Hugh Cross (Ecumenical Officer for England), Mr Douglas Fryer (Statistics Department of the Central Board of Finance), Mr Brian Hanson (Legal Adviser and Joint Registrar of the General Synod), Mr Derek Pattinson (Secretary-General of the General Synod) and the Rev. Canon H. E. C. Stapleton for answering questions and supplying information, and Mr Oswald Clark, CBE, Mr David Hebblethwaite, Mr Brian Hanson, Mr Derek Pattinson and Mr John Reddington for reading the typescript and making a number of valuable suggestions.

Rochester   PAUL A. WELSBY
August 1985

**TO
OLIVER**

I

The Establishing of the Church In England

ORIGINS

The vast amount of archaeological research which has been undertaken in the last hundred years has thrown a vivid light upon much in the early history of our country which had hitherto been unknown, but it is still far from clear how or when the Christian Church first gained a foothold in Britain. Under the Roman occupation, religion in this country varied between the gods of the official Roman religion and the variety of local deities which were the object of worship by the Celtic element in Britain. By AD 200, however, there was a considerable number of Christians in Britain. The first mention of their presence is in a tract written by Tertullian, an early Christian theologian, in about 208, in which he speaks of parts of Britain inaccessible to the Romans which had yet been conquered by Christ. Thirty years later, another Christian theologian, Origen, included Britain among the places where Christians were to be found.

In the course of time various legends and stories were circulated to explain the arrival of Christianity in this country. St Peter, St Paul, St Philip, St Joseph of Arimathaea (planting the sacred thorn at Glastonbury), have each been credited with sowing the seeds of the faith in Britain, but such stories are no more than pious inventions to account for Christianity's presence at an early date. What is probably very much nearer the truth is that the Christian faith was brought either by some of the Roman soldiers who had already been converted to Christ, or — more likely — by traders passing to Britain from Gaul. Out of the mists of uncertainty, however, there emerges the fact that in the first years of the third century, Britain produced at least three martyrs, the best known of whom was Alban. Tradition describes Alban as a soldier who, having sheltered a Christian priest, was baptized and was later tortured and beheaded at Verulamium (St Albans), in about AD 209. During the same persecution many churches were destroyed, but when it was over most of them were restored and many new ones were built.

It is clear that at this stage the Church was neither powerful nor aggressive. 'During two hundred years of life it produced no great man, built no great building, endured no serious persecution, sent out no missionaries and was obliged to appeal to Gaul for help in its internal difficulties' (H. O. Wakeman, *The History of the Church of England* (1898) pp. 1-2). It was never more than a minority religion, and of its organization and administration very little is known. It was sufficiently organized, however, to take part in the general affairs of the Church. By 314 it had at least three bishops — at London, York, and at *Colonia Londiniensium* (which is misleading, but probably stands for Lincoln or Caerleon). These three, together with a priest and a deacon, attended the Council of Arles in that year. It would seem that Christianity was fairly widely distributed over the country and that it was to a considerable extent organised into communities presided over by bishops. The fact that it experienced financial difficulties seems to indicate that it found its chief support among the poorer classes rather than among those in whose hands the wealth of the country was concentrated.

In the middle of the fourth century Christianity became the official religion of the Empire. By the end of that century the Church was becoming stronger in Britain and was finding adherents in all classes of society. No doubt every town of any size had a bishop, for at this stage of the Church's history the bishop was much more the head of the local Christian community than the administrator of a large territorial diocese. The building of churches and the founding of schools went on apace and important missionary activities were undertaken. St Ninian went to Galloway in Scotland, where in 397 he founded the first monastery in Britain; St Patrick carried the faith to Ireland in 422, where he worked for thirty years and laid the foundation of the Church to which Britain was to owe so much in subsequent years; St Iltud worked in Wales, preparing the way for the later achievements of St David.

The withdrawal of the Roman legions from Britain in 410 was followed by the series of invasions and the subsequent occupation of the country by the Jutes, Angles, and Saxons from the Continent. Large numbers of Britons retreated before these advances and withdrew to the mountains of Wales, to Devon and Cornwall, to Cumbria and Strathclyde. The result was that the British Church was cut off from Gaul and the main religious developments in Europe, for the larger part of Britain ceased to be Christian and was given over to the heathen worship of the invading tribes. The isolation of the British Church in the west of the country accounted for that disparity in structure and practice between the British Church and the rest of Europe which caused problems at a later period. Hitherto, the Church in Britain, as in the rest of Western Europe, had been predominantly an urban faith. Now in Britain it became a countryside faith, and a tribal structure and a monastic organization were substituted for the urban episcopate of Roman times.

THE ROMAN MISSION

The conversion of England (as the country may now be called) was the work of two missions, each coming from a different direction and each possessed of a distinctive character. In 597 St Augustine and a band of monks were sent to England by Pope Gregory I and landed in the Kingdom of Kent. The ruler was Ethelbert, who was married to a Christian wife. After an interview with the king outside Canterbury, Augustine and his companions were given permission to preach the Christian Gospel. Shortly afterwards Ethelbert and many others were baptized, and additional missionaries were sent from Rome. Augustine was consecrated as Archbishop of the English and set his seat at Canterbury.

When the Pope appointed Augustine as head of the English Church, he included the Celtic bishops (i.e. the bishops of the old British Church, now concentrated in the west of the land) among those who were to be subject to him. When Augustine made an approach to them, however, nothing came of it, for, in the first place, the Celtic bishops refused to recognize the authority over them of the Bishop of Rome, and, secondly, they regarded Augustine's manner as high-handed, overbearing, and inconsiderate. He, in his turn, appeared to find the Celtic bishops sulky and suspicious. Thus the Church in Britain remained divided.

THE CELTIC MISSION

One of the additional priests sent over by Gregory had been Paulinus, who was consecrated as the first missionary bishop for the north, with the title of Bishop of York. King Edwin of Northumbria, like Ethelbert in the south, was married to a Christian wife, and after a meeting of the Witan it was decided that Christianity was a better religion than the old pagan one. Edwin was baptized and the prospects for progress were good. Unfortunately, Edwin was slain in battle in 633 and Christianity was crushed in the north. In the meantime the Church had been established in East Anglia through the efforts of Felix, who was consecrated bishop and in 631 set up his seat at Dunwich.

The revival of the Christian Church in the north was the work of the old Celtic Church. Thirty years before Augustine landed in England, an Irishman named Columba had settled in the island of Iona, off the west coast of Scotland, where he founded one of the most famous of all monasteries. From this centre the Christian faith was carried to all the Northern Picts. Now Oswald, Edwin's successor as King of Northumbria, had been sent to Iona to receive a Christian upbringing and education. Not unnaturally, when he at last regained his kingdom, he turned to Iona for assistance in restoring the Christian faith. The first effort failed, but in 635 St Aidan came from Iona and made his headquarters at Lindisfarne, or Holy Island, off the coast of Northumbria. From here he went forth to convert the people. He achieved outstanding success and other missionaries (chief among them, St Chad) were also dispatched into the midlands.

THE TWO STREAMS UNITE

By the end of the seventh century there were thus two types of Christian Church in Britain. In Kent and the south there was the Roman form, valuing its connection with Rome and Europe, concerned with good order, and having as its administrative basis the territorial diocese. In the north, the Midlands, and the west was the Celtic form, isolated, loosely organized, and with a monastic, instead of a territorial, unit of administration. In addition there were differences between the two Churches about the date of the keeping of Easter and about the form of the tonsure which was the outward mark of a man in Holy Orders. The question of which type of Church order was to prevail was settled at a Council held at Whitby in 664. The Celtic point of view was powerfully represented by the great bishop Colman and by St Hilda, near whose monastery the Council was held. But the outstanding figure was St Wilfred and it was due to his efforts that the Roman point of view was adopted. Thus the English Church was both united and brought into the mainstream of Western Christianity, though not without a continuing tendency on the part of the Kings of England to a fair degree of independence so far as their relations with the Pope were concerned.

THE REFORMATION

This situation persisted until the sixteenth century when, at the Reformation, England, in protest against the theological, administrative and financial abuses of the Church, repudiated the jurisdiction of the Pope and King Henry VIII became 'supreme head' of the Church of England (modified under Elizabeth I to 'supreme governor', a title held by the Sovereign to this day). Thus the Church of England did not come into existence at the Reformation. From time immemorial, there had been a Church of England and in the middle ages it was referred to in official documents — not least in Magna Carta itself — as *Ecclesia Anglicana*. At the Reformation the Church of England retained all essential features which linked it to the Church of the early centuries — Scripture, Creeds, Sacraments and Ministry. Particular care was taken to retain episcopal ordination in the apostolic succession. The protest of the Church in the sixteenth century was against those innovations which were unknown to the early, undivided Church and contrary to the teaching of Scripture. On the other hand, the Reformation saw the Church of England affirming the sufficiency of Scripture as 'containing all things necessary to salvation', and in its public worship the reading of the Bible and the preaching of the Word were given a conspicuous position. The sacerdotal concept of the priestly office was balanced by an emphasis on its pastoral and teaching functions. Thus, the Church of England is both Catholic and Reformed. It is the same *Ecclesia Anglicana* that existed before the Reformation, purged of medieval corruptions and brought to the bar of Scripture and the Primitive Church.

II
The Province

When St Augustine came to Britain Pope Gregory proposed a scheme for the whole island when it should become Christian. England was to be divided into two provinces, with London as the seat of the primate of the southern province and York as the seat of the northern province. After the death of Augustine precedence between the two archbishops was to depend upon seniority of appointment. This scheme was never carried out. A Kentish king was supreme in south-eastern England and had established Augustine at his chief seat, Canterbury, but, although Mellitus was sent by Augustine to London in 604, Christianity took some time to establish itself there. By the time it had done so, usage had sanctified Canterbury as the archiepiscopal see. At York the Church was unable to make any settlement for many generations, much less found an archbishopric, and it was not until 735 that the see of York obtained archiepiscopal status. Thus the two provinces of Canterbury and York came into existence. In 787 the southern province was divided and Lichfield became the third archiepiscopal see. This elevation of Lichfield coincided with the powerful rise of the Kingdom of Mercia under King Offa (757-96). The arrangement did not continue long after the death of Offa and it was allowed to lapse in 803. Apart from that 16-year interlude the country has been divided into two provinces only — Canterbury and York.

Because of the failure to establish the northern province at once the Archbishop of Canterbury held undisputed sway, so that when York was established the southern archbishop considered that his primacy was sanctioned by usage and that therefore the question of seniority did not arise. York held a different opinion and in the Middle Ages there were a number of unedifying disputes over precedence until, in the middle of the fourteenth century, the Pope decided that the Archbishop of Canterbury should bear the title of 'Primate of All England', while the Archbishop of York should be styled 'Primate of England'. Today these rivalries have disappeared. The Archbishop of Canterbury takes precedence over the Archbishop of York; indeed, ranking as he does immediately after the Royal Family, he takes precedence over every subject of the Crown. The Lord Chancellor comes next and then the Archbishop of York. Nevertheless, in jurisdiction the two archbishops are quite independent of each other and the provincial decisions of the Archbishop of Canterbury have no binding effect whatsoever on the northern province. In point of fact the contact between the two archbishops is very close and in matters of importance they act in concert within their respective provinces. The term *Primate* originally indicated that the Archbishop was bishop of the 'first' or 'primary' see, but it is now applied to the chief bishop of a single state or people. Each archbishop also bears the title of *Metropolitan* which signifies that he has jurisdiction to supervise the bishops within his province. But he can only act *with* his bishops, not over against them, for he has no superior legal authority over them.

Nevertheless, the Archbishop of Canterbury is in certain respects in a special position. For consultative purposes he is regarded by the State as the Church's leading representative; he holds the privilege of crowning the monarch; he has power to grant throughout *both* provinces licences, faculties and dispensations; he may bestow academic degrees in Divinity, Arts, Law, Medicine and Music. The growth of the Anglican Communion throughout the world has meant that the Archbishop of Canterbury has great spiritual and moral authority throughout that Communion and he is President of the Lambeth Conference (see below, p.77).

When a diocesan bishopric is vacant it is the archbishop of the province who provides for the ecclesiastical administration of the diocese, usually by authorising a suffragan bishop to act on his behalf. In this capacity he is described as 'the guardian of the spiritualities' of the diocese. There are a few dioceses in which the Dean and Chapter of the Cathedral claim, or have claimed, to be the guardians during a vacancy in the see. In Durham, for example, the Dean and Chapter claim the guardianship and in fact exercise it, although the claim is formally denied by the Archbishop of York. When an archbishopric becomes vacant, the Dean and Chapter of the archiepiscopal diocese are the guardians, not the other archbishop. Normally the archbishop, assisted by other bishops, is the chief minister at the Consecration of bishops who are to serve in his province. Finally, it is to be noted that each of the archbishops, in addition to his provincial work, is the bishop of his own diocese at Canterbury and York, with all the responsibilities and duties which fall upon any diocesan bishop. The method whereby a new archbishop is appointed will be found on pp.46ff.

III
The Diocese

The diocese is the basic territorial unit of administration in the Church. In the early days of the Church a diocese normally consisted of a town and its surrounding countryside, with the bishop as the head of the local Christian community rather than as the administrative head of a large area. It was to the town with its cathedral church that the Christians in the surrounding countryside looked for their worship and pastoral care. The bishop was assisted by priests, who were his assistants at baptism and mass, and by deacons who were his chief administrative agents.

When St Augustine came to Britain, Pope Gregory's intention was that there should be 12 dioceses in Britain, but when Theodore of Tarsus was appointed archbishop in 668, sixty years after Augustine's death, there were only six dioceses in the southern province and two in the northern province — Canterbury, London, Dunwich (East Anglia), Lichfield, Dorchester, Rochester, York and Lindisfarne. In spite of much opposition, Theodore took every opportunity to divide these great bishoprics and when he died he left England with 14 dioceses — Canterbury, Rochester, London, Dunwich (Suffolk), Elmham (Norfolk, later moved to Thetford), Lindsey (Lincolnshire, later moved to Dorchester), Winchester, Worcester, Hereford, Leicester, Lichfield, York, Hexham (Durham and the southern part of Northumbria), and Lindisfarne (the northern part of Northumbria). A few years after his death the diocese of Sherborne was carved out of Winchester and the see of Selsey was created for Sussex. Two hundred years later Sherborne was divided and new sees were established at Ramsbury (Wilts), Crediton (Devon, later moved to Exeter), and Wells. In 1090 the see of Wells was moved to Bath, but a century later it was restored to Wells, and finally the diocese received the title of 'Bath and Wells', which it has retained to the present day.

During the Norman period, when Lanfranc was Archbishop, a complete diocesan reorganisation was effected and a number of sees were transferred to more populated areas. Thus, Selsey was moved to Chichester, Dorchester to Lincoln, Sherborne (in which Ramsbury had already been merged) to Old Sarum (Salisbury), Thetford to Norwich, and Lichfield to Chester. In 1095 Lichfield was moved to Coventry and in 1228 the habitual title of the see was 'Coventry and Lichfield' until the Reformation, when it was reversed to 'Lichfield and Coventry'. In 1109 a new see was established at Ely and in 1133 Carlisle was created, but from that date until the reign of Henry VIII the number of dioceses remained unaltered.

After Henry VIII had dissolved the monasteries he devised an ambitious scheme for the formation of no less than 21 new sees. In the event only six were created — at Westminster (this lasted for only ten years), Bristol, Chester, Gloucester, Oxford and Peterborough. From that period no new diocese was created until the see of Ripon was formed in 1836, to be followed in 1848 by that of Manchester. The nineteenth century saw also the creation of the dioceses of St Albans, Truro, Liverpool, Newcastle, Southwell and Wakefield. In the present century no less than twelve new sees have been established — Southwark, Birmingham, Sheffield, Chelmsford, St Edmundsbury and Ipswich, Blackburn, Bradford, Coventry, Guildford, Leicester, Portsmouth and Derby — but none in England for the last fifty years. Finally, in 1980 the Diocese of Gibraltar in Europe (usually known as the Diocese in Europe) was created by the bringing together into a single diocese of the Bishop of London's jurisdiction of English people abroad in North and Central Europe (established in 1633 and for the last ninety years exercised by one of his London suffragans) and the Diocese of Gibraltar which had included Anglican centres in territories bordering on the Mediterranean and in other parts of southern Europe.

Today there are 44 dioceses, 30 in the southern province of Canterbury and 14 in the northern province of York.

Province of Canterbury

Canterbury	Ely	Oxford
London	Exeter	Peterborough
Winchester*	Gibraltar in Europe .	Portsmouth†
Bath & Wells	Gloucester	Rochester
Birmingham	Guildford	St Albans
Bristol	Hereford	St Edmundsbury and Ipswich
Chelmsford	Leicester	Salisbury
Chichester	Lichfield	Southwark
Coventry	Lincoln	Truro
Derby	Norwich	Worcester

Province of York

York	Chester	Sheffield
Durham	Liverpool	Sodor and Man
Blackburn	Manchester	Southwell
Bradford	Newcastle	Wakefield
Carlisle	Ripon	

*including the Channel Islands
†including the Isle of Wight

THE BISHOP

Each of the 44 dioceses is presided over by a diocesan bishop, who may be appointed from 'the ranks' — in which case he will receive Consecration from his archbishop and fellow bishops — or be *translated* from another diocese or from a suffragan see. The method of appointment is described on pp.46ff.

The bishop is the head of his diocese pastorally as well as administratively. 'The diocese is not to be to him a large administrative unit which he must control, but a fellowship of parishes, the clergy and laity of which he must do his utmost to shepherd.' (C. F. Garbett, *The Claims of the Church of England*, 1947, p.97). Thus, he will be exercising his work as pastor in choosing fit men for the ordained ministry who will work in his diocese and he will, as bishop, administer to them the rite of Ordination. It is his task to appoint suitable men to the vacant benefices in his diocese where he has the right of presentation and to scrutinize those presented by other patrons. It is he who, in parishes up and down the diocese, administers Confirmation to those presented to him by the parochial clergy. This is also one of the ways in which the bishop is able to move among the clergy and laity of the diocese and to get to know them, their needs and their problems. The same is true of Institutions, when the bishop visits a parish for the purpose of instituting a new incumbent. A considerable amount of a bishop's time is occupied with preaching, not only on special occasions, but as a pastoral act on ordinary occasions in various parishes in his diocese. Many interviews and a large correspondence take up a considerable portion of most days but again these tasks are points of contact between the bishop and those over whom he presides. There is a less congenial, but none the less necessary, side to his work, namely the exercise of discipline over the clergy in the case of moral offences, neglect of duty or offences against the doctrine of the Church of England and its law of public worship. Moral persuasion, admonition, and censure are the chief means employed by the bishop in dealing with these delinquencies; very rarely is it necessary for him to take legal action against the offender.

Although the bishop is primarily the pastoral head of his diocese — the Father-in-God — he is also inevitably the administrative head. He must preside at many meetings and committees and however much he may delegate work and responsibility he is the final authority on many matters. The financial affairs of the diocese, the committees and councils guiding the various spheres of church work in the diocese, the creation of new parishes and the reorganisation of existing ones, and a hundred and one other matters, come ultimately under the responsibility of the diocesan bishop. Moreover, as the leader of the Church of England within the area covered by his diocese, he has a certain responsibility to represent the church *vis-à-vis* local secular and administrative bodies. It is obvious that in order to fulfil all these duties and obligations the bishop, unlike his absentee predecessors of past centuries, must be in close attendance upon his diocese. Nonetheless, every bishop has duties which take him, sometimes for several days at a time, away from his diocese. Three times a year, from three to four days, he must be present at the General Synod in London or York. He must be in London also for three or four one-day separate meetings of the House of Bishops and for meetings of Bishops. If he has a seat in the House of Lords (see p.48) he will have to spend two weeks in the year in London so as to read prayers in the House, quite apart from any other attendances he may be obliged to make at other times. Finally, there are meetings of the Church Commissioners and of various central committees of which he may be a member.

In all his work the bishop is assisted by his suffragan bishop (or bishops), by his archdeacons and by his rural deans. Each diocese has also its administrative and legal officers.

DIOCESAN ADMINISTRATION

Each diocese has a *Diocesan Synod*, the composition and functions of which are described on p.53. It is from the Diocesan Synod that most of the committees responsible for running the various branches of diocesan work are appointed. The most important of these is the *Diocesan Board of Finance* which is responsible for all the financial affairs of the diocese. Although it is an incorporated body, it is required to comply with such directions as may from time to time be given by the Diocesan Synod. The Diocesan Synod also appoints members to the Diocesan Pastoral Committee (which deals with the reorganisation of the parochial system), to the Diocesan Education Committee (in addition to this Committee each diocese has a full-time Director of Education) and to other bodies. To show how a diocese is administered, here is a list of the main committees in a single diocese, some appointed by the Diocesan Synod, others containing only Synod representatives, and some appointed solely by the bishop:

The Diocesan Board of Finance
The Diocesan Advisory Committee for Ministry
The Diocesan Board of Education
The Diocesan Council for Mission and Unity
Council for Social Responsibility
The Diocesan Pastoral Committee
Parsonage Committee
Board of Patronage
Advisory Committee for the Care of Churches

Redundant Churches Uses Committee
Church Music Committee
Diocesan Advisory Committee
Liturgical Advisory Committee
Association of Readers

SUFFRAGAN AND ASSISTANT BISHOPS

The title 'suffragan bishop' is applied to those bishops who are formally appointed to assist the diocesan bishop in some of his duties. During the early period of the fourteenth century it became fairly common, in the diocesan bishop's absence, to employ suffragan bishops to perform those acts which required episcopal orders (e.g. Ordination, Confirmation). As time went on it became very usual and many such bishops were appointed. Their appointment was for a limited period, they had no place in diocesan administration and they sometimes exercised their functions in more than one diocese at a time. In 1534 an Act was passed for the provision of 24 bishops suffragan, who were to take their titles from some place within the province in which they worked. This scheme was never put into full effect, for 12 of the proposed suffragan sees were never occupied and in 1592 the system lapsed. It was revived in 1870 when a bishop suffragan of Dover was appointed to assist the Archbishop of Canterbury and a bishop suffragan of Nottingham to assist the Bishop of Lincoln; and since then the number has greatly proliferated, so that today there are more than sixty.

During the last 25 years, in order to cope with the population problem and to meet the need for episcopal care, some diocesan bishops unofficially divided their dioceses into defined areas, each area being under the care of a suffragan bishop, although there have been wide differences of opinion and practice about the autonomy, if any, which can or should be given to the areas and their bishops. The Dioceses Measure 1977 established a procedure whereby a diocese can officially be divided into episcopal areas and the diocesan bishop can legally delegate certain of his powers to a suffragan bishop. Under this Measure the dioceses of London, Chelmsford, Chichester, Salisbury and Oxford have a legally established area system, the suffragan bishop in each area having the title of *area bishop*.

When a diocesan bishop requires a suffragan he nominates through the archbishop of the province two persons to the Crown, and by convention the first person named is chosen. Sometimes a bishop suffragan (or area bishop) combines with his office that of archdeacon or residentiary canon. In some dioceses there is one or more *Assistant Bishop*. In position, appointment and authority he is quite different from a suffragan bishop. An assistant bishop is one who has retired from some diocese or suffragan see but who assists in various ways, normally on a very part-time basis, the bishop in whose diocese he resides. His appointment is a private and personal arrangement by the diocesan and it ceases at the death or resignation of the latter. An assistant bishop has no territorial title. In a very few dioceses there is a full-time assistant bishop.

ARCHDEACONRIES

Every diocese (except Sodor and Man) is divided into two or more archdeaconries, each of which contain a fairly large number of parishes, presided over by an *archdeacon*. In the early days of the church the business of the diocese was performed by a staff of deacons attached to the bishop and led by the *arch*deacon, or chief deacon. The latter's particular position in the episcopal household put him in a special relation to the diocese. The first mention of the office occurs in the fourth century and the first notice of archdeacons being chosen from the ranks of the priesthood, instead of the diaconate, is in 874. Nowadays an archdeacon is always in priest's Orders. The first known holder of the office in England was Wulfstan, Archdeacon of Canterbury in 803. By the tenth century the archdeacon had acquired recognised legal status. Hitherto he had owed his position to the bishop and had taken his title from the cathedral church of which he was a member. As diocesan administration developed, single dioceses were divided into a number of archdeaconries and each archdeacon became associated with a territorial area. Since the number of dioceses has greatly increased, so the size of most archdeaconries has diminished to an area much less than that of a county.

The archdeacon is the *oculus episcopi*, the 'eye of the bishop', bringing to the latter's attention what calls for correction or merits praise. He is appointed by the diocesan bishop, he must be over thirty and have been at least six years in priest's Orders. It is part of his work to hold Visitations within his own archdeaconry at least every three years. A very ancient duty attached to his office is that of examining and presenting candidates for Ordination. The examination is now usually done by the theological college or the bishop's examining chaplains, but the archdeacon still normally presents the candidates at the Ordination Service. It is usually his task to induct a new incumbent into a benefice under the direction of the bishop after the latter has instituted the incumbent (see p.23).

The archdeacon is responsible for inspecting the fabric and contents of churches within his archdeaconry and has the power to grant a certificate for the repair of a church not involving any substantial alteration of its structure. Under the Inspection of Churches Measure 1955 powers are conferred on the archdeacon for the enforcement of the provisions of the quinquennial inspection of churches. The archdeacon is involved in certain legal proceedings in the Consistory Court of the diocese in clergy discipline cases. In these days, the archdeacon's role is increasingly seen as a pastoral one, assisting the bishop in the care of the clergy and the parishes. The Archdeacon of Canterbury, as the delegate of the archbishop, exercises the privilege of enthroning all diocesan bishops throughout the southern province. It is not known why the Archdeacon of York has no corresponding privilege in the northern province. An archdeacon is styled 'The Venerable'.

RURAL DEANERIES

Each archdeaconry is sub-divided into rural deaneries, or small groups of parishes, over which presides the *Rural Dean*. This is a very ancient office and was formerly of considerable importance. The title *decanus* signifies 'chief of ten', and it has been suggested that rural deaneries formerly corresponded with the civil groupings of parishes into 'hundreds', which were themselves commonly divided into ten sub-divisions or 'tithings'. In the early days the rural dean was sometimes known by the title *archpriest* (i.e. the chief priest in the district), and in the cathedral cities and large towns he was called 'dean of Christianity' (i.e. dean of the Christian folk). This title is still used of the deaneries of the cities of Exeter, Lincoln and Leicester. The rural dean held Chapters (i.e. meetings of the clergy of the deanery) as required, and solemn and principal Chapters were held once a quarter when all the clergy were bound to attend. All clergymen on admission to their benefices took an oath of reverence and obedience to the rural dean, who himself had important powers which were distinct and separate from the Chapter. Among these were the right of inspection and jurisdiction over all sinners in the parishes in his district, the right to censure the clergy, to visit the churches, to be custodian of vacant benefices, to induct a new incumbent, and to represent the clergy in every episcopal synod.

The office, however, fell into decay, largely because of the rise in importance of the archdeacon. The latter had originally been inferior in office to the rural dean, for he was in deacon's orders, whereas the rural dean was in priest's orders. The archdeacon, however, had the advantage of being in personal attendance on the bishop, who in course of time entrusted him with greater powers and a widening area of jurisdiction, which represented a gradual encroachment upon the rights and jurisdiction of the rural deans. In 1236 archdeacons were enjoined to be present in the deanery Chapters, with the consequence that their appearance there came to eclipse the position of the rural deans, who, resenting this, began to absent themselves.

Indeed, in some places the rural dean was nominated by the archdeacon, who also arrogated most of his powers, including that of induction of a new incumbent to a benefice. Thus the office of rural dean became obsolete. It was revived in 1836 and today the rural dean is appointed by the bishop and is a valuable channel of communication between the bishop and the parishes. In some predominantly urban areas the title 'urban' or 'area' or 'borough' dean is used.

Each rural deanery has regular meetings of the clergy within the deanery to discuss and take action on matters of common concern. This is known as the *Deanery Chapter,* and the rural dean presides at such meetings. He is also Joint Chairman (with the Chairman of the House of Laity) of the *Deanery Synod,* which consists of the clergy and lay representatives from each of the parishes within the deanery (see p.53). It is the task of the rural dean to make known to the clergy the wishes of the bishop and to represent the wishes of the clergy to the bishop.

PECULIARS

Although it is true that the bishop holds jurisdiction over the whole area covered by his diocese, there may be certain units which are exempt from that jurisdiction. These units are known as *Peculiars* and may consist of a parish, a group of parishes, or a chapel. At one time or another there have been six types of peculiar: Monastic Peculiars, where the great Abbeys and certain Religious Orders were exempt from episcopal jurisdiction; Royal Peculiars, usually where churches were situated on land connected with a Royal castle or palace (e.g. St George's Chapel, Windsor, and Westminster Abbey); Archiepiscopal Peculiars, linked with rights claimed by archbishops to exercise jurisdiction where they had manors or palaces; Episcopal Peculiars, where bishops owned residences in dioceses other than their own; and Cathedral Peculiars, in which Cathedral Chapters had jurisdiction over their property. Apart from the Royal Peculiars most of the rights and privileges of the others have now been removed, so that they now come under the jurisdiction of the diocesan bishop, although the holders of some of them retain the title of Dean (e.g. Bocking, Battle). A number of monastic foundations are still outside the diocesan bishop's jurisdiction, as also are many of the chapels of the Oxford and Cambridge colleges, although each of them has an episcopal Visitor.

IV
The Parochial System

The word *parish* comes from the Greek through the Latin. The Greek *paroikia* originally meant 'a sojourn'. It came to be applied in a spiritual sense to a local community of Christians (not to the geographical area they occupied) as to those whose true home was in Heaven and whose life on earth was but a sojourn in a foreign land. Then the word was used for the ecclesiastical area under the bishop (the modern diocese) and in the fourth century for the sub-divisions of the diocese (the parish).

It will be recalled that originally the diocese was small, with a single church presided over by a bishop and serving a town and the surrounding countryside. As the number of Christians increased it became necessary to have other church buildings beside the bishop's church, and these were normally served by a priest and deacon from the bishop's staff. This was the beginning of the movement that resulted in the development of the semi-independent parish priest. There were two stages in the process. First, there was the establishment of *minsters,* served by communities of clerics and often described as parish churches of the first foundation. They were the result of the initiative of the bishops and the central authorities of the diocese, although in England they often owed their foundation to a king or a monastery, and their purpose was to serve the Christian communities in the surrounding villages over a wide and not clearly defined area. They were, in fact, mission stations.

Secondly, there was the provision of churches serving a single village, staffed by a priest, and often described as parish churches of the second foundation. These churches were built by bishops, monasteries, or local magnates to serve individual villages on their estates. The country gradually became covered with these churches, and as their number increased so there were fewer communities for the minster to serve and the minsters thus began to die out. Some churches which were formerly minsters still bear that name (e.g. Beverley Minster, York Minster).

Those who built the churches of the second foundation and who endowed them out of their own land, not unnaturally assumed the right to choose the priest to perform the duties there. This marks the beginning of what is now known as private patronage — the right of some person, other than the bishop, to present a clergyman to serve as the incumbent of a parish. The person in whom such right is invested is known as the *patron* (see p.21). A *benefice* may be defined as the office of the incumbent — that which gives him the right to a stipend and a freehold. A *parish* is an area committed to an incumbent by the bishop for the cure (i.e. care) of souls.

The main source of the priest's revenue was *tithe,* which was the right to collect a tenth of all produce of the land and of beasts. Tithe was divided into two classes.

The *greater tithe* consisted of corn, hay and wood, and the *lesser tithe* included items like wool, pigs, milk etc. This form of revenue is the clue to a proper understanding of the difference between *rectors* and *vicars* which is a source of confusion to many people. Although the founders of the early parish churches no doubt permitted the tithe to reach the incumbent, their successors were less scrupulous and very often it is found that they took to their own use part of the tithe, according to whatever bargain they might have made with the priest they appointed. This was called 'impropriation'. Alternatively, they might, for a variety of reasons, grant it to a monastery or a cathedral. When this donation was a formal process it was known as an 'appropriation'. The parish priest who received the full income of his benefice, or the impropriating individual, or the appropriating body, were each known as the *rector*. If the church was appropriated 'in temporals' and 'in spirituals', the appropriating body was responsible for the spiritual care of the parish. Now a monastery or a cathedral could not itself exercise the care of souls and so it appointed a chaplain (*capellanus*), whose stipend and terms of service were determined by a private arrangement between himself and the rector (i.e. the appropriating body). On the other hand, if the church was appropriated 'in temporals' only, the cathedral or monastery became rectors of the parish in regard to the endowments, subject to part of their endowments being formed under episcopal authority into a vicarage for the maintenance of a priest to exercise the cure of souls. This priest was called the *vicar* — i.e. one who performed the parochial duties *vice* ('in the place of') the rector — and his emoluments usually consisted of the lesser tithes, while the rector retained the greater tithes. This somewhat complicated history explains the existence of the titles 'rector' and 'vicar', although today there is no practical difference between the two. In 1836 all tithes in kind were commuted for perpetual money payments; in turn these were redeemed in 1918 and 1936.

Thus, very early in its history the whole of the country was covered by a network of parishes, each with its parish priest — rector or vicar — and for nearly a thousand years, until the Industrial Revolution, the parochial system remained virtually unchanged. In the nineteenth century, with the rapid increase in population and the growth of large industrial towns, the existing parochial divisions were found to be inadequate. New parishes were formed and churches built in the large towns all over the country and this has continued to the present day. Since the last war, major schemes for the reorganisation of the parochial system have been put in hand and this process has been accelerated by the shortage of clergy and the constraints of finance. During this period a number of parishes and benefices have been united. A union of benefices means that the identity of parishes remains intact, each with its own parish church and parochial organisation, but their combined incumbencies become a single office, held by a single incumbent whom they share. A union of parishes involves, not only a union of the benefices of the parishes concerned, but each of the parishes loses its separate identity which is merged into a single new parish. Any proposed union of benefices and parishes is effected by a pastoral scheme under the Pastoral Measure 1983 (see p.18).

Special provision is sometimes made for the spiritual oversight of a new area of population as the preliminary to the formation of a new parish. The area may be constituted a *Conventional District* by means of an agreement between the bishop and the incumbent(s) of the parish(es) out of which the district is to be carved. By such an agreement the area is taken out of the incumbent's charge and placed under that of a Curate-in-Charge, who is given a degree of independence in ministering to the population of the area and building up the work in preparation for its legal separation. Although the residents in the district remain the parishioners of the parish from which the area has been carved, the area as a whole is able to organise itself as a distinct parochial unit, with much of the apparatus of a parish such as an electoral roll, churchwardens and a Parochial Church Council. In 1984 there were about seventy such districts in existence. The weakness of the arrangement is that in law it requires renewal with every change of incumbency in the parish or parishes in which the district is situated, although in fact this is ignored and most, if not all, continue as though nothing had happened.

THE PASTORAL MEASURE

The consolidated Pastoral Measure 1983 took the place of the Pastoral Measure 1968 and the Pastoral (Amendment) Measure 1982. These Measures have all had as their purpose the better provision for the cure of souls through the reorganisation of parishes and minsters. It enables the union of parishes to take place, parishes to be created without a parish church, the alteration of rural deanery, archdeaconry and diocesan boundaries, and the declaration of redundancy of a church building. It also provides for the creation of group and team ministries and in 1983 there were over 300 teams and some eighty groups. A *Team Ministry* is the sharing of the cure of souls in a specified area by a team of ministers consisting of the incumbent of the benefice (who is known as the team rector) and one or more other ministers (known as team vicar(s)) who have a status equal to that of an incumbent of a benefice. Other lay or ordained ministers may share in the pastoral care. The office of team rector can be either a freehold office or one held for a term of years, while that of team vicar is for a term of years only. There are special provisions for the constitution of a patronage board for the appointment of the rector of a team ministry.

Team vicars are chosen by the bishop and the rector jointly, but the Parochial Church Council and the district church councils (if in existence) must be consulted. It is the annual parochial church meeting which can elect district church councils for any area within the team.

A *Group Ministry* is where the incumbent of a benefice in the group will, in addition to attending to his own benefice, have the legal authority to assist the incumbents of the other benefices in the group. The incumbents meet as a chapter, with a chairman either elected or appointed by the bishop, and it is their duty to assist each other so as to make the best possible provision for the cure of souls throughout the area of the group. The patron of a benefice in a group cannot exercise his right of presentation until he has obtained the bishop's approval of the person he proposes to present, and the bishop has to consult the other incumbents in the group before making a decision.

Under the Measure every diocese has to have a *Pastoral Committee,* the duty of which is to review the arrangements for pastoral supervision in the diocese, having regard to the provision of the cure of souls in the diocese as a whole. Consultation with the parish is essential in making proposals for pastoral reorganisation by Scheme under the Measure and, before making any recommendations, the Committee has to seek the views of all interested parties which may be affected by a Scheme (e.g. the incumbents involved, patrons, Parochial Church Councils, local planning authorities etc.). Draft proposals then go to the bishop, who can amend them with the agreement of the Committee. They then go to the Church Commissioners and to the interested parties, after which the Commissioners prepare a draft Scheme which has to be made public. Written representations can be made to the Commissioners. During the consideration of any representations, amendments to the Scheme may be made after consultation with the diocese. The final Scheme is submitted for confirmation by Order in Council, but interested parties can then seek leave to appeal to the Privy Council.

This Measure enables a church to be made redundant. If it is no longer required for worship it can either be used for some other suitable purpose or be disposed of either as a standing building or as a site after demolition, or be maintained as a historic or architectural monument. It is the task of the Diocesan Redundant Churches Uses Committee to see if a use can be found for a redundant church. If the building is to be appropriated to a specific use, the Church Commissioners prepare a Redundancy Scheme which can empower the Commissioners to sell, or the Diocesan Board of Finance to lease, the property. If no use can be found, and if the Advisory Board for Redundant Churches, an independent body set up under the Measure, certifies that the building is of little historic or architectural interest, then, after the expiry of at least six months from the date of the Declaration of Redundancy, the Church Commissioners may prepare a Redundancy Scheme authorising the demolition of the church and the disposal of its site. If a suitable use cannot be found, and if the building, or part of it is certified to be of historical or architectural interest, then the Scheme may provide for its care and maintenance by the Redundant Churches Fund, set up under the Measure. The Redundant Churches Fund is an independent body whose function is the care and maintenance of redundant churches of historic or architectural interested vested in it by Redundancy Schemes. It is largely financed by Church and State. Approximately two-thirds of the Church's share is provided by a grant from the Church Commissioners and the remaining third from the proceeds of the sale of redundant churches and sites.

ECUMENICAL DEVELOPMENTS

The growth of ecumenical relationships and co-operation has produced alterations in the traditional parochial pattern. In the first place, the 1969 Sharing of Church Buildings Act has allowed existing Anglican church buildings to be used by other denominations and made it lawful to build new churches on a shared basis. The churches which may be parties to a sharing agreement include the Church of England, the Roman Catholic Church and all the principal Free Churches, and any two or more of these Churches may enter into a sharing agreement. In the case of the Church of England the Diocesan Board of Finance, the incumbent and the PCC of the parish concerned are necessary parties to any such agreement and the consent of the bishop and the Diocesan Pastoral Committee must be obtained. The agreement may provide for the shared building to be owned by one only of the sharing Churches or to be jointly owned by all or some of them, although an existing consecrated church of the Church of England must remain in the sole ownership of the Church of England, unless joint ownership is authorised by a Pastoral Scheme. An agreement must also make provision for determining the extent to which the building is available for worship in accordance with the forms and practices of the sharing Churches and for dealing with financial obligations as to repairs, furnishings etc.

In the late 1960s areas of ecumenical co-operation began to be established in a number of places and by 1984 there were over four hundred of these, now called *Local Ecumenical Projects* (LEPs). These are areas where, under responsible authority, certain denominational traditions are suspended for a period of years in order that new patterns of worship, mission and ministry can be undertaken. There is considerable variety of structure in these areas, but they all come within the definition in the 1975 *Guidelines for Local Ecumenical Projects,* accepted by the major Churches in

Britain, which states that 'a Local Ecumenical Project may be said to exist where there is at the level of the local church a formal, written agreement, affecting the ministry, congregational life and/or buildings of more than one denomination; and a recognition of that agreement by the appropriate denominational authorities'. Behind an LEP is a sponsoring body, which acts as a close link with the denominational authorities. Its composition depends upon the project in question, but it normally consists of official nominees of the Churches involved in the project and its object is to ensure that the experiment has the official commitment of the participating Churches, to give support and stability to the team operating the project, to guard against the project causing the establishment of a new 'denomination' and to evaluate the progress of the project. At national level there is a Consultative Committee for Local Ecumenical Projects in England (CCLEPE), which keeps in close touch with developments at local level, issues guidelines, and advises the Churches on the problems which may arise when local united action is contemplated. It is made up of two representatives from each of the major Churches, including the Roman Catholic Church, and one representative of the Free Church Federal Council. The existence of *Local Covenants,* where congregations of different denominations covenant together in the locality for mission and unity, gives rise to some confusion because they appear to be something different from LEPs. Nevertheless, the Consultative Committee for Local Ecumenical Projects in England takes the view that a Local Covenant is in fact an LEP.

GUILD CHURCHES

In the City of London there are very few resident parishioners and in 1952, under the City of London (Guild Churches) Act, fifteen of the parish churches were set aside to serve the needs of the non-resident, day-time, population of the City and ceased to have parochial status. The cure of souls exercised by the vicars of these churches is based upon an electoral roll upon which baptized members of the Church of England over sixteen years of age may place themselves without having to have residential qualifications and without losing their right to be on the electoral roll of their parish church. The clergy in charge of these churches are not incumbents having freehold, but are titular vicars, appointed for a specific number of years. They have no obligation to hold Sunday services, but exercise their ministry on weekdays, mostly during the lunch hour. Some of the Guild Churches are centres for specialist ministry.

V
The Parish: the Incumbent

The holder of a benefice is known as the Incumbent, and he may be either a *rector* or a *vicar*. The origin of these titles has already been explained (see p.16), but today they have lost their distinguishing significance. Occasionally the person in charge of a parish is called the *priest-in-charge*. This occurs when for pastoral reasons the bishop does not wish to grant the freehold, usually because pastoral reorganisation is pending in that area. The incumbent is often called the *parson*, a very ancient title dating from the eleventh century and derived from the Latin *persona* (person). According to legal writers its use stems from the view of the parson as the legal 'person' by whom the property of the parish is actually held.

APPOINTMENT
The incumbent is chosen and presented to the benefice by the patron. Just under a quarter of the benefices in England are in the gift of private patrons, including the various Trusts which hold patronage. Of the rest, about 3,700 are in ecclesiastical patronage (e.g. bishops, cathedral chapters), about 850 are in the patronage of universities and colleges and between 700 and 800 parishes are in the patronage of the Crown and its officers (including a large number to which presentation is made by the Lord Chancellor). The right to present to a benefice, if it is a perpetual right, is a right of property; the owner of such a right is said to be in possession of an *advowson*. Since 1924 it has been illegal to sell an advowson, although the patron may still bequeath it or transfer it, if neither the bishop nor the Parochial Church Council objects, to another person. Certain categories of patron, e.g. a Roman Catholic, are not allowed to exercise their right of presentation.

If a benefice is in the patronage of a Roman Catholic and is situated within the City of London or in certain counties in the Province of Canterbury, the University of Oxford exercises the right of presentation; if the benefice is in none of these places the University of Cambridge exercises the right. If the Patronage (Benefices) Measure, passed by the General Synod, becomes law every patron will be obliged to register his patronage and, after a period of 15 months, no person will be entitled to exercise the function of patron unless he has registered. Also under the proposed Measure every patron who is not a communicant member of the Church of England will have to appoint a communicant member as his representative to discharge in his place the function of a registered patron.

Since 1931, under the Benefice (Exercise of Rights of Presentation) Measure, the parishioners have an opportunity of expressing their views on the matter of the appointment of their incumbent. A vacancy in a benefice has to be notified to the

Parochial Church Council by the bishop. The council may then make representations in writing to the patron as to the conditions, needs and traditions of the parish, but without mentioning the name of any particular clergyman. In addition, the council may pass a resolution bringing into operation a particular form of machinery whereby the patron must obtain the consent of representatives of the parish for the person nominated to the vacancy. If, however, after sixty days from the bishop's original notification, a conference has been held with the churchwardens (as representing the parish) and the churchwardens have not given their consent to the patron's proposed appointment the patron may exercise his right to present after obtaining the bishop's approval of the clergyman presented as being a suitable nominee. If the bishop withholds his consent the patron may appeal to the archbishop. This Measure does not apply in cases where the Crown is the Patron.

If a patron (other than the bishop) is unable to fill a vacancy within six months the right of presentation automatically lapses to the bishop. If he fails to make an appointment within an equivalent period, or, where he is patron, he fails to fill a vacancy within six months, the presentation lapses to the archbishop of the Province and — after a further six months — to the Crown. When the patron is the Crown the right of presentation is not lost by delay and when a benefice becomes vacant by the promotion of the incumbent to an English diocesan bishopric the right of presentation to that benefice immediately lapses to the Crown for that occasion.

If the Patronage (Benefices) Measure becomes law a procedure will come into operation whereby the candidate proposed by the patron will require the approval of the bishop and of representatives of the Parochial Church Council. When a benefice falls vacant a notice of the vacancy will be sent to the patron and the PCC. The PCC will prepare a statement describing the conditions, needs and traditions of the parish which will be sent to the patron and the bishop. In addition the PCC will appoint two of its members to act as its representatives, will have the right to request the registered patron to consider advertising the vacancy, and will have the right to request a meeting with the bishop and the patron (or his representative). Whether or not such a meeting is requested, the patron will not be able to offer the vacant benefice to any priest until he has had the approval of the parish representatives and the bishop. If either the bishop or the parish representatives, or both, refuse to give approval the patron will have the right to appeal to the archbishop. If the appointment has not been made within nine months of the benefice becoming vacant, the right of patronage will lapse to the archbishop. The procedure set out in the Measure will not apply to benefices where the Crown is patron.

INSTITUTION AND INDUCTION

After a suitable clergyman has been presented to the bishop the next act is the *Institution* by the bishop into the cure of souls of the parish. When the bishop himself is the patron and presentation and institution become one act, the process is known as *Collation*. Either before or at the time of institution the incumbent-designate subscribe the Declaration of Assent. This is in two parts. The first is a Preface read by the bishop, which sets the Thirty-Nine Articles of Religion and other Church of England formularies within the context of scripture and the creeds, and which ends by asking the person making the declaration to affirm his 'loyalty to this inheritance of faith as your inspiration and guidance under God in bringing the grace and truth of Christ to this generation and making Him known to those in your care'. The second part is the Declaration itself — 'I . . . do so affirm and accordingly declare my belief in the faith which is revealed in the Holy Scriptures and set forth in the catholic creeds and to which the historic formularies of the Church of England bear witness; and in public prayer and administration of the Sacraments, I will use only the forms of service which are authorised or allowed by Canon.' The incumbent-designate also takes the Oath of Allegiance to the Crown and the Oath of Canonical Obedience to the bishop.

For the actual institution, the incumbent-designate kneels before the bishop, holding in his hand the seal attached to the Instrument of Institution while the latter is read by the bishop. The Instrument declares that the bishop admits the incumbent to the parish concerned and that he does 'in due form canonically institute you in and to the said [benefice] and invest you with all and singular the Rights, Members and Appurtenances thereto belonging . . . And we do, by these presents commit unto you the Cure of Souls of the Parishioners of the said Parish, and the Government of the Church aforesaid — your care and mine — and authorise you to preach the word of God in the Parish of — aforesaid.'

By institution the incumbent is admitted to the spiritual care of the parish. He is next put into possession of the temporalities (i.e. the property and income) of the benefice by the process known as *Induction*, which is performed by the archdeacon on the direction of the bishop. Occasionally, this is performed by the rural dean, acting as the archdeacon's deputy. The form of induction begins with the archdeacon laying the hand of the incumbent on the key or handle of the door of the church with the words: 'By virtue of this mandate I do induct you into the real, actual and corporeal possession of this church of —, with all the rights, profits, and appurtenances thereto belonging.' After this the newly inducted incumbent tolls the bell to signify to the parishioners that he has taken possession. In practice, institution and induction normally take place together in the parish church, but it is not unknown for a bishop to institute elsewhere, such as in his private chapel, and for the induction alone to take place in the parish church.

Thus, by these means, a new incumbent is put in possession of his benefice. Subject only to the rights of the bishop, he has the sole exclusive title to the emoluments appertaining to the benefice. Traditionally, these consisted of income from endowments, voluntary Easter offerings from his parishioners, and fees for marriages, burials and memorials in the churchyard. In modern times the income from these sources is augmented by the Church Commissioners and the Diocesan Board of Finance to a minimum figure recommended by the Central Stipends Authority (see p.65). Indeed, it would be more accurate to say that he is paid an annual stipend, of which receipts from fees and Easter offerings may form a part. The incumbent has a duty to reside in the parsonage house, although he may obtain the bishop's licence to live in another suitable house. He must reside in the parish for at least nine months out of the twelve. No clergyman over the age of seventy may be admitted to a benefice and normally no clergyman over that age may continue to hold a benefice (except the small number already in office prior to 1976). The bishop of the diocese may, however, on grounds of pastoral need and with the consent of the PCC, authorise his continuance in office for an extended period not exceeding two years.

When an incumbent dies, resigns, or is deprived, there is said to be an *avoidance of the benefice,* and until another incumbent is instituted *sequestrators* are appointed by the bishop to administer the parish. Until recently it was the normal practice to appoint the churchwardens of the parish as sequestrators, but other arrangements are now becoming usual. The sequestrators are responsible for providing the proper services of the church and for the payment of clergymen and readers to conduct the services. They receive the fees from marriages, burials and the erection of monuments in the churchyard and, in so far as these items are insufficient to meet their expenses, the balance will be met by the Diocesan Stipends Fund. At the close of the sequestration the sequestrators pay any balance to the Church Commissioners. Special arrangements apply when the right of presentation is suspended.

ASSISTANT CLERGY AND OTHER MINISTERS

In the execution of his duties the incumbent may be assisted by one or more curates, deaconesses or readers, or by authorised parish workers. It is to be noted that in the strict sense of the word, the incumbent himself is the *curate* of the parish for he has the 'cure (or care) of souls'. However, in common speech, the title has come to be reserved for the ordained assistant to the incumbent. A curate is licensed by the bishop and this licence confers on him a certain security of tenure. The bishop may withdraw the licence at any time, provided he has given the curate opportunity to be heard, but the incumbent has no power to end the appointment except with the bishop's consent. The curate himself, on the other hand, may resign by giving three months notice to the incumbent and the bishop. In a very few churches one of the assistant curates has the title of *lecturer,* the origin of which goes back to the appointment to particular parishes in the sixteenth and seventeenth centuries, under Puritan influence, of lecturers charged especially with preaching.

The staff of a parish church may also include a *non-stipendiary minister.* There are about 770 such priests in the Church of England today, and they are men who are ordained while continuing their secular occupation. They fall roughly into two groups. There are those who see their ministry orientated mainly towards the place where they work and there are those who see it orientated mainly towards the parish in which they live. An NSM is licensed to an incumbent or a rural dean; he receives no salary from the Church, but is entitled to any expenses incurred as the result of his work in the parish.

The origin of *deaconesses* is full of ambiguity. By the second half of the third century, however, they were recognised as standing in a special relation to the bishop as regards his dealing with women, and in the fourth century, although the relationship with the bishop was not clear, they were ordained by the bishop through the laying on of his hand. The office became obsolete in the Middle Ages, but in England it was revived to meet practical needs in 1861 and the Order of Deaconesses was formally established in 1923/25. Convocation Resolutions stated that 'the Order of Deaconesses is an Apostolic Order of Ministry in the Church of God: That the women admitted thereto are episcopally ordained with prayer and the laying on of hands.' The exact ecclesiastical status of a deaconess is, however, not easy to define; certainly she is not 'a clerk in holy orders'. The late Archbishop William Temple used to insist that a deaconess was 'a woman minister, not a female deacon'. Nevertheless, today the training of a deaconess and the duties assigned to her in a parish are indistinguishable from those of a deacon. It is for this reason that, if the Deacons (Ordination of Women) Measure, which the General Synod has approved, receives the Royal Assent, women will be admitted to the diaconate, hitherto reserved for men, and become 'clerks in holy orders'. Existing deaconesses will have the opportunity to be ordained to the office of deacon and there will be no further admissions to the Order of Deaconesses, although those already in that Order who do not wish to become deacons will remain deaconesses.

Readers are lay men and women who are appointed to perform certain functions on a part-time basis. The institution of Readers goes back in origin to the right of laymen to read the Scriptures in the Jewish Synagogue and it would appear that in the early church at the Eucharist this right continued. As time went on, in each community certain men were found especially competent to do this and so the Minor Order of Readers arose. There is evidence from the third century AD that 'the reader is appointed by the bishop's handing to him the book. For he does not have hands laid upon him'. On the other hand, there is no evidence that the reader ever conducted services, preached or engaged in pastoral work. During the early part of Queen Elizabeth I's reign the office of Reader was revived in England in order to provide religious teaching, to officiate at divine service, to bury the dead and to church women in those parishes which at that time were destitute of clergy. The office soon disappeared, until it was revived again by the bishops in 1866. It is an 'office' rather than an 'order'. Since 1969 women have been eligible for the office. A Reader is formally admitted to the office by the bishop, who presents him or her with a New Testament but does not administer the laying on of hands. A Reader is permitted to perform any of the following functions: to read Morning and Evening Prayer, to assist in certain parts of the Eucharist, to preach, to teach the children, to visit the sick, to bury the dead (if authorised by the bishop, with the goodwill of the persons responsible, and at the invitation of the incumbent), and generally to undertake such pastoral and educational work and to give such assistance to the incumbent as the latter may direct.

Men and women who have been admitted by the bishop as *lay workers* (or *parish workers*) are employed in some parishes on a stipendiary basis. Such a worker must be a communicant member of the Church of England and must have had proper training. A person who has been admitted to the office of *Church Army Evangelist* is deemed to be a lay, or parish worker. The functions of lay workers clearly resemble those of a deaconess or a reader. It is significant, however, that apart from these authorised offices, in recent years lay people have come to play an important part in the total ministry of a parish. There has been increased lay participation in the Eucharist, with laymen and women reading the lections and leading the intercessions, and laymen and women may be specially authorised by the bishop to distribute the sacred elements. Lay people have come to share with the clergy in visiting and in baptismal and marriage preparation. In many parishes 'one-man ministry' is giving place to the concept of 'shared ministry', whereby the incumbent, the assistant clergymen, the authorised lay ministers, and the ordinary laity together minister to the parish.

VI
The Parish: the Parishioners

The concept of 'shared ministry' bears witness to the fact that 'the Church' is the whole body of Christians who have been baptized, although the common fallacy that the Church is the clergy still persists. The word 'laity' is derived from the Greek word *laos*, which means 'people' and is the word used to translate the Hebrew expression 'The People of God'. By baptism a person is made a 'layman', a member of the *laos* (the People) of God — the Church — and as such the layman has his own proper responsibility in the offering of the Church's worship, in witness to the Gospel before the world, and in the government of the Church. Ministry is thus the function of the whole *laos,* both ordained and lay. The priesthood and ministry of the ordained person is not different in kind from that of every other Christian, but ordination conveys the authority of Christ in his Church to be the representative person of the Church which ordains. 'To equip God's people for the work of his service, to the building up of the Body of Christ' (Ephesians 4.12) describes the function of the ordained minister. Perhaps the most succinct statement of this relationship is that of Hans Ruedi Weber: 'The laity are not the helpers of the clergy so that the clergy can do their job, but the clergy are the helpers of the whole people of God, so that the laity can be the Church.'

Every member of the laity living within a parish has a legal right and reasonable expectation that the Services of the Prayer Book or the alternative Services authorised by the General Synod shall be performed in his own church, and every incumbent is under a legal obligation to provide Morning and Evening Prayer on all Sundays and on principal feast days and on Ash Wednesday and Good Friday. In practice, however, this is not always possible, particularly where the incumbent has two or more parishes in which to minister. The incumbent must also celebrate Holy Communion on all Sundays and greater feast days and on Ash Wednesday. Likewise, all confirmed parishioners have the right to be admitted to Holy Communion, unless the minister can show 'lawful cause' why a particular person should be refused. Every confirmed parishioner has a duty to communicate at least three times a year, of which Easter is to be one. According to Canon B15A baptised persons who are communicant members of other churches which subscribe to the doctrine of the Holy Trinity, and who are in good standing in their own church, may be admitted to Holy Communion, but if such a person regularly receives Holy Communion over a long period which appears likely to continue indefinitely 'the minister shall set before him the normal requirements of the Church of England for communicant status in that Church'.

Any parishioner has the right to have his child baptised by the incumbent, who must also go and baptise privately any infant in the parish who is ill or in danger of death. Normally speaking, all persons who are legally entitled to marry have the right to be married in the church of the parish where one of them resides or in the church where one of them has habitually worshipped for at least six months. The incumbent must refuse to marry them if one of them is not legally entitled to marry (e.g. if under the age of sixteen, if within one of the prohibited degrees of relationship, etc.) or if they have not complied with the provisions requiring banns, licence or superintendent registrar's certificate. If one of the partners has been divorced and the former partner is still living the incumbent has the right to refuse to solemnise the marriage and to refuse the use of any church of which he is the minister for such a marriage. A public service of blessing for those remarried in a Register Office after divorce is permitted in appropriate cases.

A person may be married in church only after one of the following conditions has been satisfied:

(1) *Banns* have been publicly called three times in the church of the parish (or parishes) where each of the parties resides and no impediment has been alleged. If the marriage is to take place in neither of the parishes of residence, but in the church where one of the parties has habitually worshipped and is on the electoral roll, then the banns must be called there as well.

(2) *A Licence* has been obtained which dispenses with the publication of banns. Authority to grant licences lies with the bishop of the diocese, but he delegates his authority to certain of the clergy and legal officers, who are then known as *Surrogates*. One of the parties must swear before a surrogate that there is no legal impediment to the marriage and that one of the parties, for fifteen days prior to the granting of the licence, has had his usual place of abode within the parish in which the marriage is to be solemnised or that the church in which the marriage is to take place is the usual place of worship of one of them.

(3) *A Special Licence* has been granted on the authority of the Archbishop of Canterbury, which entitles the parties to be married at any convenient place or time.

(4) *A Superintendent Registrar's Certificate* has been obtained. This is equivalent to the publication of banns, but the consent of the minister of the church must be obtained to the solemnisation of the marriage there. The certificate is granted by the Superintendent of the district in which the marriage is to take place on 21 days' notice being given.

The marriage service itself must take place only within a church licensed for marriages (most are), and between the hours of 8 a.m. and 6 p.m.

A parishioner is entitled to be buried in the churchyard of his own parish, or that of the parish where he was on the electoral roll, irrespective of the whereabouts of his death, and a non-parishioner can be buried in the churchyard of the parish where he happens to die. These rights include the interment of ashes after cremation. If a deceased person is neither a parishioner, on the electoral roll of the parish, nor has died in the parish, his burial or the interment of his ashes in the churchyard can take place only with the consent of the incumbent and churchwardens, regard being taken of the amount of space remaining for future burials. The incumbent is legally obliged to bury according to one of the authorised burial services, although he may not use that service if the dead person has not been baptised, is excommunicate, or has committed suicide while of a sound mind (*felo de se*). If it is desired to erect a monument or tombstone in the churchyard, the consent of the incumbent is always necessary and it is his duty to ensure that no memorial of undesirable size, shape or design is erected and that no unsuitable inscriptions are permitted. If unusual monuments are proposed, a Faculty (see p.34) must be obtained.

Fees are payable in the case of marriages, burials and the erection of monuments. The Church Commissioners frame an Order establishing a table of fees to apply to every parish and this is subject to approval by the General Synod, which has no power to amend the Order. Draft legislation recently approved by the General Synod and awaiting parliamentary consideration will, if enacted, give the General Synod power to amend a draft Order, subject to the Church Commissioners having the right to withdraw it for further consideration in the light of any amendments. An order also requires parliamentary approval by the 'negative resolution' procedure whereby unless a 'prayer' to annul the order is moved and carried it is deemed approved after a period of forty days.

The forms of service to be used in the parish church are regulated by the Church of England (Worship and Doctrine) Measure 1974. Under the Measure the 1662 Book of Common Prayer must continue to be available for use. With regard to the services in the Alternative Service Book, 1980, and other authorised alternative services, the decision as to which form of Morning and Evening Prayer and Holy Communion is to be used in the parish has to be taken jointly by the incumbent and the Parochial Church Council. If they are unable to agree the forms to be used are those in the 1662 Prayer Book, except that if another approved form of service has been in regular use in the Church for at least two years in the past four years, then the Parochial Church Council may require that form to be used. In the case of the occasional offices — baptism, marriage and funeral — the choice of the form of service lies with the minister who is to conduct the service, although any lay person concerned is entitled to register a preference beforehand. If the minister and the person concerned are unable to agree, the matter must be referred to the bishop for decision. In the case of Confirmation and Ordination, the bishop decides which of the alternatives is to be used. If legislation at present before the General Synod becomes law, the bishop will be obliged to make the decision after consulting the minister of the church where the service is to be held.

The Prayer Book (Versions of the Bible) Measure, 1965 provides that where any portion of Scripture (including the Psalms) is appointed by the Prayer Book to be read or sung, the corresponding portion of Scripture contained in any version of the Bible for the time being authorised for the purpose by the General Synod may be substituted. This may be done at the discretion of the minister, provided that the Parochial Church Council agrees, or, in the case of the occasional offices, provided none of the persons concerned objects beforehand to its use. The same rules apply to the biblical passages — psalms, readings and sentences — in the Alternative Service Book. The versions at present authorised for this purpose are the *Authorised Version,* the *Revised Version,* the *Revised Standard Version,* the *New English Bible,* the *Jerusalem Bible, Today's English Version* (the *Good News Bible*), *The Revised Psalter* and *The Psalms: a New Translation for Worship* (usually known as *The Liturgical Psalter* and printed in the Alternative Service Book).

VII
The Parish: Councils and Officers

PAROCHIAL CHURCH MEETING

A *Parochial Church Meeting* is held annually in every parish not later in the year than 30th April. All persons who are on the *Electoral Roll* of the parish are entitled to attend and vote. This Roll contains the names of all those lay persons who are baptised, who are members of the Church of England or of a Church in communion with the Church of England, who are 16 years of age upwards, and have signed a form of application for enrolment. They must be residents in the parish or they must have habitually attended public worship in the parish during six months prior to enrolment. The Roll has to be revised annually and an entirely new Roll prepared every six years. The Electoral Roll is of importance not only as being the nominal roll of electors to the Parochial Church Council, but also as the basis for lay representation in other tiers of Synodical Government (see Chapter XI).

At the Annual Parochial Church Meeting three types of business are transacted:

(1) *Reports* — The Meeting receives from the Parochial Church Council a copy of the Electoral Roll, a report on the year's proceedings of the Council and on the financial affairs of the parish, a copy of the audited accounts for the preceding year, a report on the fabric, goods and ornaments of the church, and a report on the proceedings of the Deanery Synod. The accounts have to be approved by the meeting and, if they are, signed by the chairman, and the Parochial Church Council must cause them to be published and affixed to the door of the church.

(2) *Elections* — The Meeting elects lay members of the Parochial Church Council, sidesmen and, in every third year, parochial representatives of the laity to the Deanery Synod. Election may be by show of hands or by ballot. The Meeting also appoints the auditors for the Council.

(3) Any person entitled to attend the Meeting may ask any questions about parochial or general church matters or bring about a discussion of such matters by moving a general resolution or by moving to give any particular recommendations to the Parochial Church Council. The PCC is not bound by the passing of any such resolution, but it must give full consideration to what is resolved or expressed by the Annual Meeting.

In addition to the Annual Meeting a special Parochial Church Meeting may be convened if occasion should demand. The chairman of an Annual Meeting is normally the incumbent, or, in his absence, the vice-chairman of the Parochial Church Council, or, if he also is absent, a person chosen by the Meeting.

THE PAROCHIAL CHURCH COUNCIL

The Parochial Church Council is the chief administrative body in the parish and its existence ensures that the laity of the parish have a voice, jointly with the incumbent, in the affairs of its church. Membership of the Council consists of:

(1) The incumbent

(2) *Ex officio* members: — licensed clergymen (including team vicars in the case of a team ministry); any deaconess or lay worker; the churchwardens (being communicants); any lay member of the Deanery Synod, Diocesan Synod or General Synod whose names are on the roll of the parish.

(3) Such, if any, of the Readers whose names are on the roll of the parish, as the annual Meeting may determine.

(4) Members (who must be actual communicants of seventeen years of age or upwards) elected by the annual Meeting.

(5) Co-opted members (who must be either clerks in Holy Orders or lay communicants), not exceeding one-fifth of the elected representatives.

With the prior permission of the bishop, a member of another Church which subscribes to the doctrine of the Holy Trinity, who is baptised, of communicant status, of good standing in that Church, and who is an habitual worshipper and communicant at the parish church, may be nominated for election to the Parochial Church Council, provided he is aged 17 or over.

The incumbent is the *chairman,* a lay member of the Council is elected *vice-chairman* and the Council appoints a *secretary* (who need not be a member of the PCC) and a *treasurer.* An *electoral roll officer* must be appointed, but need not be a member of the Council and may be the secretary. The *Standing Committee* of the Council, which has power to transact business between meetings, consists of the chairman, the churchwardens and at least two members appointed by the Council from among its own membership. The Council must meet at least four times a year and it has power to appoint committees to which it may nominate persons who are not members of the Council.

The scope of the work of the Parochial Church Council is much more than administrative. Its essential task is to co-operate with the incumbent 'in promoting in the parish the whole mission of the Church, pastoral evangelistic, social and ecumenical'. Its functions also include 'consideration and discussion of matters concerning the Church of England or any other matter of religious or public interest'. It is the duty of the incumbent and the Parochial Church Council 'to consult together on matters of general concern and importance to the parish' (Synodical Government Measure, 1969, Sec.6).

The Parochial Church Council is a body corporate with perpetual succession and, therefore, has a legal existence apart from the members who compose it. Its main powers and duties can be summarised as follows:

(1) The supervision of the financial affairs of the church and the keeping of accounts.

(2) The power to frame an annual budget of money collected for the church and to take such steps as it thinks necessary to raise money for such purposes. It has a duty, jointly with the incumbent, to determine the objects to which all monies collected in church, except at Holy Communion (see p.35), are to be given.

(3) The care, maintenance, preservation and insurance of the fabric of the church and its ornaments, together with the care and maintenance of the churchyard. The Inspection of Churches Measure 1955 provides that a church must be inspected by a qualified architect at least once in every five years. After the inspection the architect makes a report on the church, one copy of which is sent to the PCC.

(4) The power to acquire, manage and administer property for ecclesiastical and educational purposes.

(5) The power, jointly with the incumbent, to appoint and dismiss the verger, parish clerk and sexton and to determine their salaries and conditions of service. The Council should be joined as a party to any agreement between incumbent and organist for the purpose of guaranteeing the organist's salary and, if legislation at present before the General Synod becomes law, the agreement of the Parochial Church Council will be required before the incumbent can appoint the organist or terminate his employment.

(6) The power to make a voluntary *Church Rate* for any purposes connected with the affairs of the church. The Rate can be levied only on parishioners who are members of the Church of England and since 1868 payment is entirely voluntary. In fact, this power is rarely, if ever, used.

(7) The Council can claim the right to be consulted in the appointment of a new incumbent (see pp.21ff). Under the proposed Patronage (Benefices) Measure (see p.22) the Council will appoint two parish representatives who, with the patron and the bishop, will be consenting parties to any appointment to the benefice.

(8) The Council has an important voice in any decisions as to the use of forms of service authorised under the Church of England (Worship and Doctrine) Measure 1974 (see p.29).

(9) Under the Pastoral Measure 1983, the Parochial Church Council of any parish which is liable to be affected by a proposed Pastoral Scheme is an 'interested party' whose views must be ascertained at each stage (see p.18).

(10) Under the Parsonages Measures 1938-47 the Council is entitled to object to a proposal for the sale or demolition of the parsonage house.

(11)   The Council is responsible for making known and putting into effect any provision made by the Diocesan or Deanery Synod and it may also give advice to and raise any matter with the Diocesan and Deanery Synods.

FACULTIES

Although the Parochial Church Council is responsible for the care and maintenance of the fabric and furniture of the church, the parish church and its contents do not belong to any one generation of parishioners. What is done, therefore, to its fabric and contents is of much wider concern than to the present inhabitants of a parish. Moreover, the fabric and furniture of the church are in the ultimate guardianship of the bishop, and it is because of this that the law forbids any alterations to be made in the structure or ornaments of the church except those approved by the bishop's legal representative. Therefore, before structural alterations in the fabric (other than routine repairs) can be made, and before any of the existing fittings can be removed or new ones installed, it is necessary to have permission and that permission is given by means of the grant of a *Faculty* by the Chancellor of the diocese after formal Petition has been made. The Petition is usually made in the name of the incumbent and church-wardens, although in fact any parishioner may make it. It is lodged in the Consistory Court of the diocese, where objections may be made. If these are not sustained, or none is raised, a Faculty is issued. If work is done without a Faculty it is open to any parishioner to apply for a Faculty authorising the removal of the work.

In every diocese there is an Advisory Committee for the Care of Churches, consisting usually of experts in architecture, archaeology and art, together with the archdeacons and representatives of clergy and laity, whose function is to assist the Chancellor in deciding whether a Faculty shall be granted. In the case of repairs not involving substantial alterations in the structure the archdeacon may issue a certificate authorising the work, in lieu of a Faculty.

Much of the present procedure will change when statutory effect is given, as is intended, to recommendations in the recent report, *The Continuing Care of Churches and Cathedrals,* 1984.

CHURCHWARDENS

The chief lay officers of the parish are the *churchwardens* and this ancient office is a reminder of the days when the parish was not only an ecclesiastical area but also a unit of civil administration to a far greater extent than it is today. The office began as that of a purely ecclesiastical official. The general custom of the Church of England placed certain duties upon the parishioners as a whole, such as the repair of the nave of the church; such duties meant that from time to time the incumbent had to call the parishioners together and not unnaturally the discharge of these various duties was delegated by the parishioners to representatives. It would appear that these representatives were occasionally summoned by the bishop to his episcopal synod to give information concerning disorders amongst the clergy or people. By the thirteenth century the office, under the title of 'churchwarden', emerged with legal recognition. These officers were charged with the maintenance and repair of the church fabric and the provision of all the requisites necessary for divine service, and they were responsible for raising money for this purpose. It was also their task to beg or buy the malt and brew the liquor for the Church Ales, which were the medieval counterpart of the later parish socials. Certain charitable bequests were administered by the churchwardens, who were also responsible for law and order in the churchyard. In 1603 it was laid down that churchwardens 'shall diligently see that all the parishioners duly resort to their Church upon all Sundays and Holy Days'.

With these important officers available it is not surprising that the central government used them to enforce locally various administrative and legal measures. Thus, they often came to hold the office of overseers of the poor, and were associated with the constable in the administration of the statutes connected with ale houses, vagrancy, profane swearing and the observance of the Sabbath. Today these civil and administrative duties are no longer discharged by the churchwardens, whose functions are once again solely ecclesiastical and may be summarised as follows:

(1)   It is their duty to maintain order in church and churchyard, especially during times of service. They may remove persons who cause a disturbance or show that they intend to do so. It is an offence punishable by law to cause any disturbance in the church or to interrupt divine service and the churchwardens have the power to arrest any such disturbers.

(2)   It is the churchwardens' duty to provide seats in the church for the parishioners, and they may direct persons where to sit, and where not to sit.

(3)   The churchwardens (jointly with the incumbent) are responsible for the disposal of money collected at Holy Communion. The Parochial Church Council (jointly with the incumbent) is responsible for money collected at other services.

(4)   When a vacancy occurs in the benefice, the churchwardens are sometimes appointed sequestrators (see p.24). As representatives of the Parochial Church Council they may be consulted by the patron in the appointment of a new incumbent (see p.22).

(5)   The churchwardens are the officers of the bishop and it is their duty, on the bishop's or archdeacon's visitation, to answer such questions as may be put to them about the condition of the parish. They should also at any time report to the bishop any irregularity or failure of duty of which he ought to be informed.

There are usually two churchwardens in each parish. They must be either resident in the parish or on the electoral roll of the parish and, unless the bishop permits otherwise, must be actual communicant members of the Church of England. They are appointed by the joint consent of the incumbent of the parish and a meeting of the parishioners. 'Meeting of parishioners' means a meeting of the persons whose names are on the church electoral roll of the parish together with the persons resident in the parish whose names are entered on the register of local government electors. In practice this meeting is usually held immediately before the annual Parochial Church Meeting. If agreement cannot be reached then the incumbent may appoint one and the parishioners the other. The churchwardens should be chosen not later than 30th April in each year. Before entering on their duties they must be formally admitted to office and this takes place at the bishop's or archdeacon's Visitation, one of which occurs each year, when they must subscribe the declaration that they will faithfully and diligently perform the duties of their office. No person chosen for the office of churchwarden is able to exercise his office until he has been admitted in this manner.

The churchwardens are assisted in their duties by *sidesmen* (which include women) elected by the Annual Church Meeting.

OTHER PAROCHIAL OFFICERS

In a few parishes there is a *parish clerk*. In theory this office may be held either by a layman or by a person in Holy Orders, but in fact it is normally held by a layman (or woman). Traditionally, the parish clerk assisted the priest at divine service, chiefly by making the responses for the congregation and sometimes by reading the Epistle at Holy Communion. Today the parish clerk is more or less synonymous with the verger (see below). In the Middle Ages the more menial duties of the parish clerk, including the care of the church and churchyard, the digging of graves and the care of the ornaments of the church, were performed by the *sexton*, but today the latter's duties are confined to grave digging and the parish clerk's other duties are performed by a *verger* (or *virger*). The parish clerk and sexton, where the offices survive, are appointed jointly by the Parochial Church Council and the incumbent. The *verger* is employed by the Parochial Church Council. The strict meaning of the title is the official who carries a 'verge' (from the Latin *virga*), or mace, before a dignitary, and such in fact was the origin of the office. Nowadays he is a 'jack of all trades', caring for the interior of the church and acting as the general servant of the minister and churchwardens in carrying out work in the church. The office of *organist* requires no explanation. He is appointed and dismissed by the incumbent. If legislation before the General Synod becomes law the function of appointing the organist and of terminating his employment will be exercised by the incumbent with the agreement of the Parochial Church Council. In the case of termination, however, the Archdeacon may consider that the circumstances are such that the agreement of the Parochial Church Council may be dispensed with.

VIII
The Cathedral

What makes a church a cathedral is not its size, age, splendour or geographical position, but the presence within it of the bishop's seat or chair, for which the Greek name is *cathedra*. The church may be small or large, ancient or modern, in a large town or off the beaten track, but if the bishop's seat is in it it is the cathedral of the diocese. Because the cathedral possesses the bishop's chair, two things follow. In the first place, because the bishop's throne is the visible symbol of his pastoral and teaching authority and jurisdiction, the cathedral is the principal church of the diocese over which that pastoral and teaching authority and jurisdiction extend. Secondly, because it is the mother church of the diocese, it has always been the aim to make the cathedral pre-eminent as a place of worship. To secure this, colleges or foundations of priests and others were established and endowed for the purpose of maintaining the worship of God. This leads to another important definition of a cathedral. It is not only a building; it is also a society — a society of dean and canons, minor canons, singing men and boys of the choir, vergers and other officials. It is a society devoted to the offering of worship, to preaching, education, music and mission.

It has already been shown (see p.7) that in the early days the bishop gathered round him in the church where he had his *cathedra,* a group of priests which formed a community under his rule and whose task it was to assist him in the celebration of the Liturgy and the Offices and to act as his advisers and administrators. From this primitive organisation arose the regularly constituted *dean* and *chapter* of post-Conquest times. Gradually the cathedral became independent of the bishop. There were several reasons for this. As the bishop's responsibilities increased and his jurisdiction expanded and as the worship of the cathedral church became more elaborate, so responsibility for the administration of the cathedral was gradually delegated to the chapter. In time the latter became an independent ecclesiastical corporation, a process accelerated by endowments made to the cathedral independently of the bishop. The bishop thus came to have less authority over his own cathedral church than over any other church in his diocese, although he could still use it for synods, visitations, ordinations and confirmations. He also had the duty of formally 'visiting' his cathedral from time to time and of deciding disputes over the interpretation of the cathedral statutes. This is still, broadly speaking, the position today in the majority of cathedrals.

About a third of our cathedrals were established before the Reformation in the sixteenth century. They were of two kinds. There were the 'secular' ('secular' meant 'non-monastic') cathedrals with their Chapter of dean and canons. Three of the latter, known as *dignitaries,* were given the titles and offices of precentor, chancellor and treasurer. The *precentor* was the director of the music and the ceremonial observancies in the cathedral and he had as his assistant a *succentor* (or sub-chanter). The *chancellor* presided over the theological and educational work of the cathedral, and his assistant was the *vice-chancellor*. The *treasurer* was entrusted with the care of the furniture, sacred vessels, plate etc. of the cathedral and was assisted by the *sub-treasurer* (occasionally known as the *sacrist*).

The dean and chapter of the secular cathedrals followed a common rule of life, but although in this respect their routine resembled that of the monastic rule they were not members of a religious order. There came into existence, however, another type of cathedral that was served, not by a group of secular priests, but by a monastic community. This type of cathedral was, in effect, a monastic church which, because it possessed the bishop's 'cathedra', was also the mother church of the diocese. Here there was no dean or canons. The bishop was the titular abbot of the monastery, but the real head of the cathedral was the prior of the convent and the worship and the administration of the cathedral were performed by the monks.

At the Reformation the secular cathedrals, with their deans and canons, were left undisturbed. They were known as *Cathedrals of the Old Foundation* and have continued until today. When Henry VIII, however, suppressed the monasteries this included the monasteries whose churches were also cathedrals. Of these, Coventry and Bath ceased to be cathedrals. The remainder continued to function but, instead of being served by monks, they were reorganised somewhat along the lines of the secular cathedrals with deans and canons. At this time, also, new cathedrals were established at Chester, Bristol, Gloucester, Oxford and Peterborough to serve newly-created dioceses and they too were given a constitution on the secular model. Both the converted monastic cathedrals and the newly-established cathedrals were known as *Cathedrals of the New Foundation*. After this no new cathedral was established until the nineteenth century, but since then the increase in the number of dioceses has seen a corresponding increase in the number of cathedrals.

This somewhat lengthy historical essay has been necessary in order that we may understand the differences in the constitution and nomenclature of the cathedrals today. The Cathedrals of England can be divided into three groups:—

(1) *The Cathedrals of the Old Foundation* — served from the first by a college of secular priests, developing into a chapter of dean and canons, remaining more or less unchanged at the Reformation. These Cathedrals are Chichester, Exeter, Hereford, Lichfield, Lincoln, London (St Paul's), Salisbury, Wells and York.

(2) *The Cathedrals of the New Foundation* — the cathedrals established or re-established by Henry VIII after the dissolution of the monasteries. These fall into two groups:—

(i) Those which prior to the dissolution were cathedrals governed by monks and were afterwards converted to a secular constitution. They are: Canterbury, Carlisle, Durham, Ely, Norwich, Rochester, Winchester and Worcester.

(ii) Those which before the Reformation were not cathedrals at all. They are: Bristol, Chester, Gloucester, Oxford and Peterborough.

(3) *Modern Cathedrals* — These are all churches which have become cathedrals since the middle of the nineteenth century, and they fall into two groups:—

(i) Previously existing parish churches raised to cathedral status. They remain parish churches as well as being cathedrals. They are: Birmingham, Blackburn, Bradford, Bury St Edmunds, Chelmsford, Derby, Leicester, Manchester, Newcastle, Portsmouth, Ripon, St Albans, Sheffield, Southwark, Southwell and Wakefield.

(ii) New Cathedral buildings — These are Coventry, Guildford, Liverpool and Truro.

Today, in the cathedrals of both the Old and the New Foundations much the same organisation prevails, the main difference being that of terminology. In both cases, at the head of the chapter is the dean, who is appointed by the Crown. Associated with him are the *residentiary canons* of which there are usually four, two of which are to be engaged exclusively on cathedral duties. In the cathedrals of the Old Foundation the ancient offices and titles of precentor, chancellor and treasurer have been retained. The residentiary canons live in the cathedral precincts and each is 'in residence' for a certain number of months in each year. In some instances one or more of the residentiary canonries is annexed to an archdeaconry and at Oxford and Durham canonries are allotted to certain professorships in the university.

Next, there are attached to each cathedral a number of canons who receive no emoluments and who do not reside in the cathedral precincts. They are chosen by the bishop of the diocese and are appointed as a mark of honour for outstanding merit, for long and faithful service to the diocese, or because of the possession of some particular office in the diocese. In cathedrals of the New Foundation and in modern cathedrals they are called *honorary canons* (in some cases *non-residentiary canons,* as at Peterborough, or *canons diocesan,* as at Liverpool) and are a comparatively modern 'invention' dating from 1840. In the case of some of the cathedrals of the Old Foundation they retain the ancient title of *prebendary.* Formerly the latter received his emoluments from the possession of an estate (or *prebend,* so called because it supplied or furnished — *prebere* — a living to the holder) but today, like an honorary canon, he receives no emoluments (since 1840).

At Canterbury, there is, in addition to the honorary canons, a body of priests known as *The Six Preachers*. These were established when Canterbury became a secular Cathedral in 1542 and the Preacher was required to deliver sermons in the cathedral on Saints' Days and in the parish churches which stood on lands owned by the chapter. They lived within the cathedral precincts and were provided with horses for their journeys to the outlying parishes. Today they are non-resident but preach once a year.

In most cathedrals the dean and residentiary canons form the *Cathedral Chapter*, which is the body responsible for the spiritual and temporal concerns of the cathedral church. This is known as the Administrative Chapter. The Greater Chapter consists of the dean, residentiaries and honorary canons (or prebendaries). Every cathedral is subject to the Cathedrals Measure 1963 and each has its own Constitution and Statutes, agreed by the Cathedrals' Commission, laid before Parliament and confirmed by the Privy Council.

Most of the Modern Cathedrals are, in addition to being cathedrals, parish churches. Moreover, they do not possess the endowments of the more ancient cathedrals. For these two reasons, their Constitution is quite different from those of the cathedrals of the Old and New Foundations, and there is also considerable diversity between one cathedral and another. Normally, the head of a parish church cathedral bears the title of *provost*. The title is of ancient origin for as early as the ninth century a new office was created in the cathedrals of Worcester and Lichfield, where a viceregent of the bishop was appointed under the title of provost. Some parish church cathedrals, however, have adopted the older title of dean. The provost or dean of these cathedrals is also incumbent of the parish and, except in the case of Bradford and Sheffield, is appointed by the bishop. There is a Cathedral Council containing representatives of the congregation, but the amount of administrative responsibility allotted to the Cathedral Council varies from cathedral to cathedral.

After the Civil War and until the latter part of the nineteenth century the cathedrals of England went through a period of profound neglect and dilapidation. In the last seventy-five years, however, they have been reformed, cleaned and restored. We may conveniently end this chapter with a note on the place of the cathedral in the life of the Church today.

(1)   It is the mother church of the diocese and in this capacity it is the place where services particularly associated with the bishop are held. Chief among these are the ordination services and other great diocesan occasions. Parties, groups and individuals from all over the diocese are welcomed at the cathedral where they are invited to see the treasures of the building and to join in the cathedral worship. The

canons of the cathedrals are often on the staff of the diocese as well and, in that capacity, go out to the parishes on various activities. The cathedral choir may visit parishes and the cathedral organist will often give advice and assistance to organists and choirs in the parishes.

(2) The cathedral has a special relationship with its immediate neighbourhood. It will have links with local government, schools, colleges, hospitals and social services. It will sometimes provide services, music or discussion groups in the lunch hour for workers in the city.

(3) The cathedral is increasingly a place of pilgrimage and every cathedral has its evangelistic and educational opportunities among the mass of sightseers and the many chance worshippers at its services. In order to welcome pilgrims and to help them as much as possible a number of cathedrals have provided ancillary facilities such as gift shops, guides in various languages, visitors' centres, treasuries, refectories, exhibition areas and car parks.

(4) The cathedral itself remains a community of persons — dean (or provost) and chapter, choristers and lay clerks, sometimes a school — a community of persons in Christ. It is this community which enables the cathedral to remain a centre where continuous and reverent worship is offered to Almighty God. In most cathedrals Holy Communion is celebrated and Morning and Evening Prayer are said or sung daily. So the continual round of prayer and praise is maintained. Emphasis is laid on order and decency in worship and a choral foundation exists to provide the best of music, with the result that in most of the cathedrals there is a high standard of music and order in worship, which can be an example to the whole diocese.

IX
The Non-Parochial Ministry

In addition to the bishops and to the clergy in parishes and on cathedral foundations, there are a considerable number of ordained men who are engaged on
'specialist' work of one kind or another, most of whom bear the title of *chaplain*.
There are also the men and women who are members of the *Religious Orders*.

CHAPLAINS

Originally a 'chaplain' was a priest who had charge of a chapel, but today the title
is ordinarily given to a clergyman who performs non-parochial duties whether he
has the charge of a chapel or not. It is difficult to draw up a comprehensive list of
the various types of chaplains in the Church of England. They may, however, be
roughly divided into two groups — those which are State appointed and those
which are not.

Chaplains who are appointed and paid by the State are Chaplains to the Armed
Forces, Prison Chaplains and Hospital Chaplains. The Chaplains' Branch of the
Royal Navy is administered by the Chaplain of the Fleet, who holds the dignity of
Archdeacon under the Archbishop of Canterbury. Naval Chaplains do not hold any
naval rank, but 'retain when afloat the position to which their office would entitle
them on shore'. They are employed in sea-going ships, in Naval dockyards at home
and abroad, in Naval and Marine barracks, hospitals, colleges and other Naval
establishments. Queen's Regulations and Admiralty Instructions provide that
morning prayers should be said on weekdays in HM Ships and Establishments with
the usual services on Sunday. The Naval Chaplain is also concerned with all aspects
of the spiritual welfare of those over whom he is appointed.

In the Army, chaplains hold commissioned rank and are under the Chaplain-
General to the Forces (who has the title of archdeacon) at the Ministry of Defence.
Regular chaplains are charged in Queen's Regulations with 'providing by all prac-
tical means the spiritual and moral welfare of the troops'. At Bagshot Park in
Surrey there is the Royal Army Chaplains' Department Training Centre and Depot
which serves as a spiritual home for all chaplains. There are also Territorial Army
Chaplains who serve TA units in their locality on a part-time basis. In the Royal
Air Force the head of the Chaplains Branch is the Chaplain-in-Chief (who has the
title of archdeacon). Chaplains to Prisons and Borstal Institutes are appointed by the
Home Secretary and are under the authority of the Chaplain General of Prisons
(who has the title of archdeacon). Hospital Chaplains are appointed by a Health
Authority following interview by a Health Authority Appointments Committee,
which includes assessors appointed by the Diocesan Bishops and by the Hospital

Chaplaincies Council. Under Ministry of Health Regulations a full-time chaplain may be appointed in a hospital where there are 750 patients or more of the denomination concerned. Otherwise, except under special circumstances, the appointment is a part-time one and is made by a Health Authority which requests the Diocesan Bishop for a suitable nomination.

Apart from these State appointments there is a variety of chaplains independent of the State. Most colleges at Oxford, Cambridge and Durham have their own college chaplain. Many of the modern universities and polytechnics now have an Anglican chaplain, either on a full-time or part-time basis. In the majority of these cases the appointment lies with the church authorities of the diocese in which the university or polytechnic lies. Every Church of England College of Education has its chaplain, who is also usually a college lecturer. There are a number of independent schools that have a chaplain, who may be the local incumbent. Alternatively, it may be a full-time appointment, in which case the Chaplain usually teaches in class in the same way as any other member of staff.

Since the last war the development of industrial mission has seen the appointment in most dioceses of industrial chaplains, full-time and part-time. The appointment is made by the bishop and penetration into particular industries has to be earned by the chaplain and it is as he meets men regularly, as individuals and in groups, that he becomes accepted by both workers and management.

Among the non-parochial clergy must be included the ordained staffs of the Theological Colleges, priests working on behalf of various Church Societies, Charities and Trusts, those employed by the Boards and Councils of the General Synod, and those on the staff of religious broadcasting departments. It is reckoned that the total number of full-time non-parochial clergy is in excess of 2,000.

THE RELIGIOUS ORDERS

Within the last hundred years there has been a considerable revival and development of the Religious Orders in the Church of England. From the early days of Christianity the monastic life has been one of the features of the Church and wherever, in those days, Christianity spread the monasteries spread too. During the early Middle Ages the great monastic orders (such as the Benedictine and the Cistercian), the orders of canons regular (such as the Augustinians and the Pre-monstratensians) and the friars (such as the Franciscans and the Dominicans) flourished and spread. The members of the Religious Orders lived according to a specific rule, usually under the three vows of poverty, chastity and obedience. Prayer was their central activity, but many also engaged in farming, education, art, the care of the sick and the practice of hospitality. It would not be easy to exaggerate the debt which England owed, spiritually, educationally and economically to the monasteries. But as time went on the situation changed. They became corrupt, they ceased to fulfil any useful function, their missionary zeal evaporated, as centres of learning and education they declined, and many of them were in financial difficulties. Because of these facts, because many of them belonged to foreign orders exempt from local episcopal jurisdiction, and because they tended to be strong supporters of the Pope, the monasteries in England were dissolved after the breach with Rome in the sixteenth century and many of their buildings were destroyed.

In the three centuries following the Reformation there were no more monks, nuns or friars in England. The first signs of the revival of the religious life occurred in 1845 when the first Anglican sisterhood, the Society of the Holy Cross, was established at Park Village, London. The first real attempt to start the religious life for men was the founding by Joseph Leycester Lyne (who later took the name of 'Brother Ignatius') of the first Benedictine monastery since the Reformation at Claydon, near Ipswich, in 1863. Although the Order persisted for many years it never received the official approbation of the Church of England. In 1865 the first monastic foundation for men which endured and became recognised by the Church was formed by several people under the direction of R. M. Benson, vicar of Cowley, under the title of St John the Evangelist, Oxford. Earlier two other communities for women had been established, the Community of St Mary the Virgin at Wantage in 1849 and the Community of St Margaret at East Grinstead in 1854. Since then there have been many new orders founded, so that today there are in the British Isles some ten communities for men and some forty-five for women.

The work undertaken by the communities includes service in the Church overseas, teaching, care for the sick and the elderly, the training of clergy, land cultivation, work with the homeless, drug addicts and delinquents, printing and craftsmanship of many kinds. Thus much active work is undertaken by the Religious Orders. Nevertheless, the chief duty of every Religious Community is to maintain the life of prayer and worship among its members. The constant stream of prayer and worship which rises from the communities is a most potent force supporting the daily work of the Church. They have been described as the spiritual power houses of the Church of England.

The Advisory Council on the Relations of Bishops and Religious Communities was established in 1935 to advise bishops on questions arising about the rules of existing communities and about the establishment of new communities, and to advise communities and their visitors. The Chairman is a diocesan bishop appointed by the two archbishops.

X
Church and State

In official documents the Church of England is described as 'by law established'. The phrase is misleading for, although the Church of England is the established church of the land, one will search in vain for any Act of Parliament or Deed of Trust formally establishing it in the same way as other Churches have been legally recognised since the Toleration Act of 1689. The Sovereign, who must be in communion with the Church of England, is the 'Supreme Governor' of the Church of England and in the Coronation Oath promises to uphold 'the Protestant reformed religion established by law' and to 'maintain and preserve inviolably the settlement of the Church of England, and the doctrine, worship, discipline and government thereof, as by law established in England'. The position of Supreme Governor does not entitle the monarch to discharge any spiritual functions, for as Article 37 of the Thirty-Nine Articles makes clear, 'we give not to our Princes the ministering either of God's Word, or of the Sacraments'. Moreover, under present constitutional practice the monarch is unable to act without the advice of her ministers.

Establishment does not mean that the Church is identified with the State nor that it is a department of State operating under a Ministry for Religious Affairs. 'The particular characteristics of the Church of England are what constitute the relationship which goes by the name "establishment". These particular characteristics embrace both "rights and privileges" and, on the other hand, "restrictions and limitations", and it is not always easy to distinguish between them. The status of "establishment" includes the restriction to Anglican clergymen of the office of Chaplain to the Speaker of the House of Commons and certain professorships and chaplaincies in the universities of Oxford, Cambridge and Durham; the right of the Archbishop of Canterbury to crown the Sovereign; precedence in all religious services associated with events of importance in the national life; the representation of the Episcopate in the House of Lords; the requirement that the Sovereign must join in Communion with the Church of England; the right of the parish priest to celebrate marriages recognised as lawful, and his position as "persona" of his parish and not merely as minister of a gathered congregation.' (*Church and State: Being the Report of a Commission appointed by the Church Assembly*, 1952, p.7.). To this it may be added that the establishment of the Church includes the incorporation of the law of the Church within that of the realm and the public recognition of the Church's Courts and Judges as possessing a proper legal jurisdiction.

Such are 'the rights and privileges' of establishment. The remainder of this chapter will be mainly concerned with 'the restrictions and limitations'. It is important, however, to emphasise that although the Church of England has this close connection with the State it is nevertheless essentially the Church of Christ, holding its commission neither from the Crown nor from Parliament, but from Our Lord himself.

APPOINTMENT OF BISHOPS

Bishops of the Church of England are appointed by the Crown but under present constitutional practice, because the Monarch acts only on the advice of her ministers, it falls to the Prime Minister of the day to submit a name to the Crown for appointment. Until 1977 no procedure was laid down for the choice of names for nomination, though normally the Prime Minister through his Secretary for Appointments sought advice from those who had knowledge of the needs of the vacant diocese and who knew also the potentiality of possible candidates for office. However, a shroud of mystery surrounded these proceedings and there was considerable criticism of a process which denied the Church a formal part in the choice of its own chief pastors. In 1977, after consultation between the Church and the Prime Minister and the leaders of the other main parties, the General Synod established a Crown Appointments Commission, which consists of 12 members — the two Archbishops, three members elected by the House of Clergy of the General Synod and three elected by the House of Laity, together with four members appointed by the vacancy-in-see Committee of the vacant diocese. The Prime Minister's Secretary for Appointments and the Archbishops' Secretary for Appointments are *ex officio* but non-voting members.

The vacancy-in-see Committee of the diocese is composed of the suffragan bishop or bishops, the dean or provost of the Cathedral (or, if he is unable or unwilling to serve, a residentiary canon), one of the archdeacons, the proctors elected by the diocese to the Lower House of Convocation and the members elected by the diocese to the House of Laity of the General Synod, the chairmen of the Houses of Clergy and Laity of the Diocesan Synod, and not less than two clergymen and two lay persons elected by the House of Clergy and the House of Laity of the Diocesan Synod. Two additional persons, one clerical and one lay, may be nominated by the Bishop's Council to represent a special interest in the diocese. The task of the Committee is to draw up a statement setting out the needs of the diocese and providing factual information about the diocese, to discuss possible candidates for the vacant see and to elect its four representatives on the Crown Appointments Commission.

The Archbishop of Canterbury is Chairman of the Commission when an appointment in the Province of Canterbury is being considered and the Archbishop of York presides when an appointment in the Province of York is being considered. In the case of an appointment to the archbishopric of Canterbury the chairman is a communicant lay member of the Church of England appointed by the Prime Minister. For the appointment of an Archbishop of York the chairman is a communicant lay person appointed by the Standing Committee of the General Synod. When an appointment is to be made to Canterbury the Secretary-General of the Anglican

Consultative Council is invited to attend as a non-voting member. If in relation to any matter a vote is required, the question shall not be deemed to have been carried unless it receives a two-thirds majority of the total voting members of the Commission and the Chairman must be satisfied that the vote in favour pays due regard to the opinions of the diocesan members. The Commission agrees upon two names for submission to the Prime Minister which may be placed in order of preference, but the Prime Minister has the right to take the second name or to ask the Commission for a further name or names. It is true that the final submission of a name to the Crown continues to lie with the Prime Minister and not with the Church but, because of the status of the Sovereign as Supreme Governor of the Church of England (which the Church had no wish to change) and also because of the constitutional position that the Sovereign can only act on the advice of his ministers, the position of the Prime Minister had to be retained. What needs to be borne in mind and may be of greater significance, is that the present system rests on a political convention or 'gentlemen's agreement' and not on law. The appointment of the Bishop of Gibraltar in Europe falls outside the scope of the Crown Appointments Commission and is made by a procedure laid down in the Measure establishing the diocese in 1980.

After a bishop has been nominated by the Crown, the procedure is as follows:

(1)   The Sovereign forwards to the Dean and Chapter of the Cathedral of the diocese the *congé d'élire*, which is the licence giving them permission to elect. The licence is accompanied by a Letter Missive from the Sovereign, containing the name of the man chosen by the Crown and instructing the Chapter to elect him. If it should refuse to elect, the Sovereign can proceed to appoint by Letters Patent. In fact the Chapter invariably does elect the Royal nominee.

(2)   The Crown instructs the archbishop of the Province to confirm the election and, if the candidate is not already in episcopal orders, to consecrate. By convention, which seems to go back at least to the reign of Charles II, the Vicar General of the province holds a court for the purpose of confirming the election, other than the election of an archbishop, which by statute is carried out by a Commission of bishops.

(3)   The archbishop consecrates the new bishop, other bishops assisting, and it is then that he is admitted to the episcopate.

(4)   The newly appointed and consecrated bishop is enthroned in the Cathedral church of his diocese. This ceremony possesses no legal significance, but it marks the ceremonial and public entry of the new bishop into his Cathedral and diocese.

(5)   Either before or after enthronement the bishop pays homage to the Queen, after which he is able to possess the temporalities (i.e. the income and property) of his see.

BISHOPS IN THE HOUSE OF LORDS

From the earliest times bishops were summoned to National Councils, where they sat with the great nobles. They probably owed their presence there to the fact that they were territorial 'magnates' and held land from the King. For the Model Parliament of 1295 and regularly afterwards writs were sent to the archbishop and bishops. At the same parliament seventy abbots and priors were also summoned and, although their number fell, they continued to receive a summons until the surrender of the monasteries at the Reformation. Since the Reformation the bishops have continued to hold seats in the House of Lords but in 1847 it was enacted that however many bishops there might be their seats in the House of Lords should never exceed 26 i.e. the two archbishops, the three senior bishops (London, Durham and Winchester) and 21 others according to the seniority of their appointment. One of their number takes prayers in the House each day at the opening of sittings. Some bishops attend only rarely, but the majority like to attend when they can and on certain occasions they make valuable contributions to debate. Some have expert knowledge on particular subjects, all can express the views of the Church on religious and moral issues involved in Government policy, and as many ecclesiastical matters find their way to Parliament it is important that the Church should be represented there. Parliamentary participation in debate is one of the ways in which the Church expresses and exercises its mission to the people and society of England.

OTHER CROWN APPOINTMENTS

The Crown appoints to all suffragan bishoprics, to all deaneries, to some resident-iary canonries and to a large number of benefices. The Crown also has the right to present to all benefices vacated by reason of the incumbent being appointed to a diocesan bishopric. All bishops, incumbents and curates must take the oath of Allegiance to the Crown before consecration, institution or ordination.

THE CHURCH'S WORSHIP AND DOCTRINE

Until recently no change could be made legally in the doctrine or worship of the Church of England without the express sanction of Parliament. The Book of Common Prayer itself forms a schedule to the 1662 Act of Uniformity. The

Church of England (Worship and Doctrine) Measure 1974, however, authorised the General Synod to make its own provisions for forms of service without recourse to Parliament. There is one condition — the Book of Common Prayer must continue to be available for use until the Synod brings a further Measure to Parliament for its discontinuance. With that one exception, the Church of England now has freedom to order its own worship. For a new service to be authorised it must have a two-thirds majority in all three Houses of the General Synod and for a new service, so authorised and excluding the occasional offices, to be used in a parish there must be agreement between the incumbent and the Parochial Church Council (see p.29). The Measure also gives the Synod power to make provision concerning the obligations of the clergy and others to assent or subscribe to the doctrine of the Church of England.

THE STATE AND THE CHURCH'S LEGISLATION AND COURTS

Until 1919 legislation affecting the life of the Church had to pass through Parliament like any other statute and the vast increase of Parliamentary business in the nineteenth century meant that very little time could be devoted to ecclesiastical legislation. Thus, time and again, ecclesiastical needs were blocked by Parliament. For example, out of 217 Church Bills introduced into the House of Commons between 1880 and 1913 only thirty-three were passed; 162 were never discussed at all. By passing the Church of England Assembly (Powers) Act 1919, usually known as the Enabling Act, Parliament delegated to the Church Assembly (a body already constituted by the Church), and in 1969 to the General Synod, most of its legislative authority in ecclesiastical affairs. Nevertheless, ultimate legislative control remains with Parliament, for when a Measure has passed through all its stages Parliament can still debate it and must either accept or reject it. The General Synod can, without reference to Parliament, pass canons which, when duly enacted and promulged, form part of the law ecclesiastical, but even here the Church is not free to do as it likes, for canons cannot be embarked upon without a Royal Licence and when made must receive the Royal Assent, which the Sovereign can give only on the advice of ministers. Moreover, the Convocations cannot meet except in response to a Royal Writ and, as the General Synod comes into being on the calling together of the Convocations, the Crown, constitutionally advised, could prevent the Convocation and, therefore, the General Synod, from meeting. The sentences of the Ecclesiastical Courts (see Chapter XIV) are enforceable by the State and the final Court of Appeal, in cases which involve neither doctrine nor worship, is a secular court — the Judicial Committee of the Privy Council, sitting usually with ecclesiastical assessors.

XI
Synodical Government

ORIGINS

Synodical Government in the Church of England came into operation in 1970. Before then there were two sets of national ecclesiastical bodies:

(1) *The Convocations of Canterbury and York,* which are entirely clerical bodies dealing primarily with matters affecting doctrine and worship. In origin the Convocations are the oldest legislative bodies in England having greater antiquity than Parliament itself. They had the right to make canons, which were binding on the clergy. The Convocations could meet only if summoned by Royal Writ, were unable to make canons without Royal authority, and such canons as they did promulge required the Royal Assent before they became operative.

(2) *The Church Assembly,* which came into existence as a result of the Enabling Act of 1919. Prior to the passing of this Act the law affecting the Church could be altered only by Act of Parliament. The Church Assembly was a body composed of the two Convocations together with a House of Laity elected by the laity of the dioceses. It dealt primarily with administrative and financial matters, but it also possessed legislative powers uniquely delegated to it by Parliament, and Measures, passed by the Assembly under these powers after resolutions being passed by both Houses of Parliament and having received the Royal Assent, had the force of statute law.

In the course of time certain weaknesses in this system became apparent. There was, first, a considerable amount of overlapping so that some business was transacted in the Convocation of Canterbury, in the Convocation of York and in the Church Assembly. Secondly, the system was time-consuming, particularly for the bishops and clergy who had to attend Convocation twice or three times a year and the Church Assembly three times a year. Thirdly, the Church Assembly, consisting of some 750 members, was too large a body for satisfactory debate. Fourthly, because matters of doctrine and worship were the proper business of the Convocations, the laity (represented only in the Assembly) had no participation in discussions and decisions on these matters. Fifthly, the Assembly was remote from the dioceses and parishes. It was not only to remedy these weaknesses, however, that a new form of Church government was inaugurated by the Synodical Government Measure 1969, but also because of new theological insights into the nature of Church Government.

The basis of Synodical Government is to be found in a report of 1902:—

'That theology justifies and history demonstrates that the ultimate authority and right of collective action lies with the whole body, the Church, and that the co-operation of clergy and laity in Church government and discipline belongs to the true ideal of the Church'. *(The Position of the Laity in the Church).*

The result of Synodical Government is that all matters affecting the Church, including doctrine and worship, come before one body instead of three and this means that the laity have full participation in such matters. Secondly, the General Synod (about 556 members) is considerably smaller than its predecessor (about 750 members), and this leads to better debate. Thirdly, less time is involved for, although the General Synod meets three times a year, the Convocations (which still exist) meet but rarely. Fourthly, there is a much closer link between the General Synod and the dioceses and the parishes. This is achieved in two ways. First, the election to the House of Laity of the General Synod is made by members of Deanery Synods instead of, as under the old system, by Diocesan Conferences. Secondly, certain Measures have to be sent to Diocesan Synods for approval before a final decision can be made by the General Synod, and on other important matters the dioceses are consulted, and many of these issues are passed down by the Diocesan Synods to Deanery Synods.

THE SYNODICAL STRUCTURE

1. *The General Synod* discharges six types of business:

(1)   It is a *legislative body* promoting Measures affecting the life and work, the finance and administration of the Church which, when they have passed through all their stages, have the force of statute law. A Measure comes before the General Synod for General Approval and it then goes to a Revision Committee. This is followed by a Revision Stage in the Full Synod and then, usually after a final tidying up process, the Synod gives Final Approval. The Measure is then sent to the Legislative Committee of the Synod, which sends the Measure, with explanatory comments, to the body known as the Ecclesiastical Committee. The latter is a Parliamentary body, consisting of 15 members of the House of Lords nominated by the Lord Chancellor and 15 members of the House of Commons nominated by the Speaker. Its duty is to scrutinise the Measure to see that it contains nothing which affects adversely the constitutional rights of the citizen and to make to Parliament a report on the nature and effect of the Measure and its views as to its expediency. If the Committee reports favourably a resolution is moved in each House of Parliament recommending that the Measure be presented to the Queen for the Royal Assent. Parliament has no power to amend a Measure, but can debate it and reject the resolution. When a Measure has passed these various stages and has received the Royal Assent it has in all respects the status and effect of an Act of Parliament.

(2) It is a *liturgical body* which, under the Church of England (Worship and Doctrine) Measure 1974, has the function of providing forms of service for use in church.

(3) It is a *financial body,* responsible for financing the central administration of the Church.

(4) It is a *deliberative body* which acts as a forum for:—

(a) expressing Christian views and insights on major public issues, political, economic, social and moral.

(b) discussing and settling central Church business, such as matters affecting the ordained and lay ministry, education and church schools, church membership, church discipline and church buildings.

(c) monitoring the relationship of the Church of England with other Churches at home and abroad, notably with the other Provinces of the Anglican Communion and with the Anglican Consultative Council, and with the national and international ecumenical bodies of which the Church of England is a member, such as the World Council of Churches, the Conference of European Churches and the British Council of Churches. It is under this aspect of its work that church unity schemes, ecumenical co-operation and working arrangements with other Churches are initiated and decided.

Decisions in the General Synod are normally made by a majority of the whole Synod, but if 25 members demand it a vote by Houses has to be taken and the motion fails unless passed in all three Houses. On some matters a vote by Houses is mandatory and on certain issues a two-thirds majority in each House is required. Under Article 8 of the Constitution of the General Synod a Measure or Canon providing for permanent changes in the service of Holy Baptism or Holy Communion or in the Ordinal, or a scheme for constitutional union or a permanent and substantial change of relationship between the Church of England and another Christian body in this country, cannot receive final approval without prior endorsement by a majority of the Diocesan Synods and without securing a two-thirds majority vote in each of the three Houses of the General Synod. Under Article 7 of the Constitution a provision concerning doctrine or worship, before receiving final approval, must be referred to the House of Bishops and receive final approval in terms proposed by that House. Such matters may also be referred to the Convocations and/or the House of Laity for separate consideration if these bodies decide to exercise this right.

2. *The Diocesan Synod* discharges five types of business:—

(1) It considers matters concerning the Church of England and makes provision for such matters in relation to the diocese.

(2) It is a forum for the expression of Christian opinion on any matter of religious or public interest.

(3) It advises the bishop on any matter on which he may consult the Synod.

(4) It deals with matters specifically referred to it by the General Synod and can also refer matters up to the General Synod.

(5) It makes provision for the financing of the diocese.

Every Diocesan Synod must, by its standing orders, establish a *Bishop's Council* to advise the Bishop, to act as the standing committee for the Diocesan Synod, and to discharge on behalf of the Synod the functions referred to above. The membership of the Bishop's Council is laid down by standing orders of the Synod.

3. *The Deanery Synod's* task, as officially defined in the Synodical Government Measure 1969, is to 'generally promote in the deanery the whole mission of the Church, pastoral, evangelistic, social and ecumenical'. To this end it brings together the views of the parishes of the deanery on common problems, discusses and formulates common policies and fosters a sense of community and inter-dependence among those parishes. It can consider and express an opinion on any matter of religious or public interest. It deals with matters specifically referred to it by the Diocesan Synod and, in the process, may sound parochial opinion on the issues before it. It can send resolutions for debate in the Diocesan Synod.

4. *The Parochial Church Council* (see page 32).

THE MEMBERSHIP OF THE SYNODS

1. The basis of the electoral system is the *Electoral Roll* (see page 31).

2. At the *Annual Parochial Church Meeting* there are elected the representatives of the parish to serve on the Deanery Synod.

3. The *Deanery Synod* consists of two Houses:

    (i) The House of Clergy (i.e. all the Clergy beneficed or licensed in the deanery, clerical members of the General Synod or Diocesan Synod resident in the deanery, and one retired clergyman chosen by and from among the retired clergy resident in the deanery).

(ii) The House of Laity (i.e. those elected by the parishes at the Annual Church Meeting, lay members of the General Synod or diocesan synod who are on the electoral roll of a parish in the deanery, and deaconesses and full-time lay workers in the deanery).

4. The *Diocesan Synod* consists of three Houses:—

(i) The House of Bishops (i.e. the diocesan bishop and the suffragan bishops).

(ii) The House of Clergy (i.e. clergymen elected by the clergy of the deanery synods, the dean or provost of the cathedral, the archdeacons, the proctors for the clergy in the General Synod and certain other *ex officio* members).

(iii) The House of Laity (i.e. lay persons elected by the houses of laity of the deanery synods, the lay representatives of the diocese in the General Synod and certain other *ex officio* members).

5. *The General Synod* consists of three Houses — the House of Bishops, the House of Clergy and the House of Laity. It is necessary at this point to make mention of the Convocations of Canterbury and York, for these bodies, although they no longer have the power to make canons, still maintain a separate existence and meet occasionally. Each Convocation still consists, as before, of an Upper House of Bishops and a Lower House of Clergy. The House of Bishops in the General Synod is composed of the combined membership of the Upper Houses of the two Convocations, and the House of Clergy is composed of the combined membership of the Lower Houses of the two Convocations. Election of the clergy is therefore election to a Convocation and it is by that route that they find themselves members of the General Synod. They are known as 'proctors' for the clergy. The chief officer of the Lower House of each Convocation is the *Prolocutor* and each Prolocutor is chairman, or vice-chairman, in yearly rotation, of the House of Clergy of the General Synod. Each archbishop is the President of his Convocation, and the two archbishops are joint presidents of the General Synod. With this in mind, we can set out the membership of the General Synod as follows:—

(1) The House of Bishops (i.e. the Upper Houses of the two Convocations), consisting of all the diocesan bishops, together with nine representatives elected by the suffragan bishops from among themselves.

THE CHURCH'S LEGISLATIVE BODIES

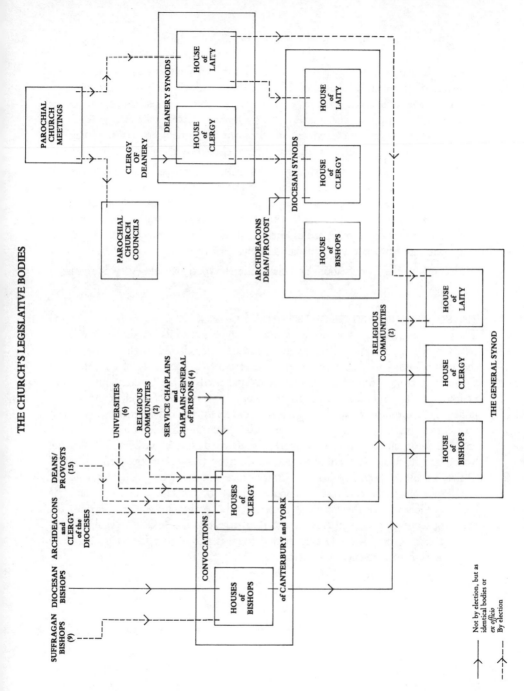

(2) The House of Clergy (i.e. the Lower Houses of the two Convocations), consisting of 15 representatives elected by the deans and provosts from among themselves, one archdeacon from each diocese, the three Chaplains-General to the Forces, the Chaplain General of Prisons, six representatives of the clergymen in the universities, two representatives of the ordained members of the religious communities, and proctors from each diocese elected by the clergy of that diocese.

(3) The House of Laity, consisting of representatives from each diocese, elected by the lay members of the deanery synods of those dioceses, three representatives of the lay members of religious communities, and a number of *ex officio* members (e.g. the Dean of the Arches, the three Church Estates Commissioners and the Chairman of the Central Board of Finance, provided they are laymen). The House of Laity appoints its own chairman and vice-chairman.

Elections to the Convocations and the General Synod are held every five years.

THE STANDING COMMITTEE OF THE GENERAL SYNOD

The continuing work of the General Synod is monitored by its Standing Committee, which is a body of some thirty members, the majority elected by the Synod, under the chairmanship of the Archbishop of Canterbury. The tasks of the Standing Committee are to keep under review the overall needs of the Church and to make proposals to the Synod for appropriate action, to advise the Synod on matters of policy, to co-ordinate the work of the Synod and its Boards and Councils, to plan and monitor the business for meetings of the Synod, to ensure that decisions of the Synod are carried out, and to continue the work of the Synod between sessions. The General Synod and its Standing Committee are serviced by the staff of the General Synod Office, led by the Secretary-General. Other officers of the Synod, in addition to the two Prolocutors, the chairmen and vice-chairmen of the House of Laity, and the Secretary-General, are the Financial Secretary, the Assistant Secretary-General, the Standing Counsel, the Legal Adviser and Registrar, and the Assistant Legal Adviser.

After each session of the General Synod there is published a *Report of Proceedings* which is akin to Parliament's *Hansard*.

XII
The Boards and Councils of the General Synod

The General Synod has four main advisory bodies:—

(1) *The Advisory Council for the Church's Ministry* (ACCM), which, although it is a Council of the Synod, has also direct responsibility to the bishops in respect of some of its functions. The Council is responsible for promoting the most effective forms of accredited ministry, ordained and lay, and for making recommendations for this purpose to the bishops and to the Synod, and for encouraging the support of candidates for Holy Orders, for women's ministry, and for other forms of accredited lay ministry. It is responsible for arranging selection conferences at which selectors, appointed by the bishops, can assess the candidates for ministry, and for keeping under review the different forms of training for ordained and lay ministry. It has the task of advising on methods of training and testing of candidates and of advising on the location, establishment, inspection and financial support of theological colleges and other courses of training. It advises dioceses on patterns of post-ordination and in-service training for the ordained and lay ministry. Finally, it co-ordinates the work of accredited lay ministry in the dioceses.

The Council has eight sub-committees:— Accredited Lay Ministry, Candidates, Finance and Grants, Readers, Theological Education, Courses and Examinations, Continuing Ministerial Education, and Vocations and Publications. There is a link between ACCM and the *Central Readers' Conference,* which is the successor of the Central Readers' Board, which came into existence in the nineteenth century. The Executive Committee of the Readers' Conference is also the Readers' Committee of ACCM. The Conference exists to further the work and ministry of Readers and it publishes a quarterly magazine, *The Reader.*

(2) *The General Synod Board of Education* is responsible for the promotion and co-ordination of the work of the Church of England in education and its concerns are divided into three areas, each under the general oversight of a committee responsible to the Board. *The Schools' Committee* deals especially with matters concerning church schools, although it also seeks to co-operate in religious education generally, including that given in the county schools. Its work is carried out in close connection with the National Society (see p.58) and the two bodies have the same Chairman, General Secretary and Administrative and Schools Officers. The Committee communicates with the Department of Education and Science on matters relating to schools and maintains close links with the professional and educational bodies and with the education departments of other Churches. *The Education and Community Committee* is concerned with the involvement of the

Church in voluntary education outside the formal structure of school and college. It is responsible for servicing the diocesan agencies of the Church in this area and it seeks to promote ecumenical endeavours in voluntary education. The children's work of the Committee is concerned with ministry to children outside school hours. In its youth work it seeks to meet the educational and social needs of young people between the ages of 14 and 21, irrespective of religious affiliation. The Committee's adult work embraces general adult education, specifically Christian education, and lay training. *The Higher and Further Education Committee* aims to develop the Church's presence and witness in these fields. It is concerned with the Church Colleges of Education and with Chaplaincies in Higher Education, including polytechnics. One of its main tasks, however, is to analyse and reflect upon the changes in emphasis and direction within the national education system and to offer advice to and to stimulate action by the Church in response to these changes. There is also a *Publications Committee* of the Board.

This is an appropriate point to refer in more detail to the *National Society,* which is not one of the Councils of the General Synod but was founded by Joshua Watson and others in 1811 and incorporated by Royal Charter in 1817. Its full title was 'The National Society for the Education of the Poor according to the principles of the Church of England'. It was a pioneer in the provision of elementary education for the children of this country before there was any system of State education. A new Charter, granted in 1934, extended the objects of the Society to include 'the promotion, encouragement and support of religious education in accordance with the principles of the Church of England among all our subjects living in England and Wales, irrespective of age or degree'. Until the foundation of the Church of England Council for Education in 1947, the Society was recognised as the Church's central organisation concerned with education.

Although since 1947 the society has not been responsible for defining or stating the Church's official educational policy it has retained its responsibility and freedom to express its views, born out of long experience, on any aspect of religious education. It gives its fullest support to Church Schools and Church Colleges of Education and it distributes grants for the building and repair of Church Schools. Like the Board of Education, it concentrates 'upon the importance in Church Schools and Colleges of the content of religious education in accordance with the principles of the Church of England as set forth in the Book of Common Prayer and the Church Catechism'. The Society manages a number of educational Trusts, provides an information service on legal and other matters for school managers, teachers, etc., and keeps a register of Church teachers to assist those reponsible to obtain well-qualified members of the Church to teach in their schools. One of the

Society's main works is the production and publication of literature for religious education. There is close liaison with the Schools Committee and the Higher and Further Education Committee under the Board of Education.

(3) *The Board for Mission and Unity* exists to advise the General Synod and the dioceses on the Church's responsibility for mission and unity and to further the links between the Synod and the Anglican Consultative Council, the individual provinces and dioceses of the Anglican Communion and the United Churches incorporating former Anglican Provinces. It is the principal channel of communication between the Synod and the World Council of Churches, the Conference of European Churches, the British Council of Churches and all other Churches at home and abroad. Finally, it is the link between the Synod and the Missionary Agencies and the Partnership in World Mission (see p.78). The Secretary-General of the Anglican Consultative Council or his representative and the Secretary of the BCC Division of Ecumenical Affairs are Consultants to the Board, which is also represented on the Consultative Committee for Ecumenical Projects in England (see p.20). The Board is closely involved in enabling the Church of England to share fully in the Partners in Mission exercises (see p.78). Other aspects of the Board's work can be seen from the functions discharged by its four sub-committees. *The Faith and Order Advisory Group* advises the archbishops and the Board on any matters of ecumenical or theological concern referred to it by the archbishops or the Board. *The Committee on Roman Catholic Relations* exists to promote relations between the Church of England and the Roman Catholic Church in this country. *The Home Committee's* task is to 'stimulate responsibility in diocese and parish for the mission and unity of the Church at home and overseas'. It is the main channel of communication between the Board and the local churches. Finally, *The Inter-Faith Consultative Group* acts as a link between the Board and the British Council of Churches' Secretariat for Relations with People of Other Faiths. It advises the Board on inter-faith questions and provides a forum for information, exchange and co-ordination between Church of England agencies which are concerned with relations between peoples of different faiths.

(4) *The Board for Social Responsibility's* work covers a wide range of social issues affecting both domestic and international affairs. Through its committees, advisory groups and working parties it engages in detailed studies of aspects of life in society. The Board has three Standing Committees. *The Industrial and Economic Affairs Committee* is concerned with the promotion and encouragement of the development and understanding of the relevance of Christian theology to the ethics of industrial

society, the maintenance of relationships at the national level with such bodies as the Trade Unions, Employers' Associations and Government Departments, the encouragement of study of the problems and opportunities of modern industrial society and the provision of training arrangements for those who intend to undertake full-time work on behalf of the Church in industry. *The International Affairs Committee* promotes studies and discussions that will contribute to Christian thinking on international relationships. As well as having the task of informing the Board on aspects of international relationships which require consideration by the Board and the Synod, it is also the channel of communication between the Board and both the Commission of the Churches on International Affairs of the WCC and the Division of International Affairs of the British Council of Churches. This Committee is also involved in *The Overseas Settlement,* which advises and assists members of the Church of England who may be going overseas and also provides for people to be met and welcomed on arrival overseas. *The Social Policy Committee* is concerned with legislation and other developments in the fields of social policy and practice, including the health and social services, social security and housing. It also considers aspects of sexuality, marriage and the family.

In addition to these Standing Committees, the Board has four Advisory Bodies. The first, *The Development Affairs Committee,* is concerned with world development. The second, *The Prison Chaplains' Advisory Group,* advises the Board on matters relating to prison chaplaincies and penal affairs. The third, *The Environmental Issues Reference Panel,* deals with matters connected with the environment. The fourth body is *The Race, Pluralism and Community Resource Group,* whose concern is with community and race relations, relations with people of other faiths and relations between white and black led churches. The Board also produces a quarterly journal, *Crucible.*

There are a number of other central bodies of the Church of England to which reference must be made, but this is not an exhaustive list.

(1) *The Central Board of Finance* was incorporated in 1914, and in 1921, after the setting up of the Church Assembly, had its duties extended to act as the financial executive to that body. In 1970 the Board became the financial executive of the General Synod. In this role it is responsible for the management of the financial business of the Synod and this includes 'the administration of money voted by the Synod for Boards and Councils and for other purposes, the presentation of an annual report and accounts and of the preparation of an annual budget . . . As the financial advisory body of the Church of England the Board is charged with

responsibility for advice and co-ordination over the finances of the Church as a whole'. It is also concerned to emphasise the importance of Christian stewardship. The income of the Board comes from contributions from the dioceses, each of which has a representative on the Board (see also p.67).

(2) *The Church of England Pensions Board* is the successor of the Clergy Pensions Institution set up in 1886 and was constituted by the Church Assembly in 1926 to serve as the pension authority for the Church of England. The Board is responsible for pensions and retirement accommodation for all who retire from full-time ministry and of their widows. It is directly accountable to the General Synod and works in close co-operation with the Church Commissioners, whose general fund now bears almost all pension costs. The Chairman of the Board is appointed by the General Synod and the Board itself consists of 21 other members, 16 of whom are elected by the General Synod and 5 nominated by the Church Commissioners. The Board owns and manages eight residential homes (a ninth is under way) and one nursing home. There is close co-operation between the Board and the dioceses.

(3) *The Council for the Care of Churches* was originally established to co-ordinate and assist the work of Diocesan Advisory Committees (see p.34) and in 1972 it became a permanent Commission of the General Synod. It advises the Synod on the contribution and care of churches and their contents and provides Diocesan Pastoral Committees (see p.18) with information on the architectural and historic merits of churches likely to be declared redundant. It acts on the Synod's behalf in negotiations with government departments and professional bodies over church inspection and repair.

(4) *The Cathedrals Advisory Commission for England,* established in 1949, assists and advises cathedral deans and chapters on plans and problems affecting the fabric and furnishings of cathedrals. It became a permanent Commission of the General Synod in 1981.

(5) *The Crown Appointments Commission* (see p.46).

(6) *The Dioceses Commission,* set up in 1978, considers proposals prepared under the Dioceses Measure 1978 for the reorganisation of diocesan boundaries, the creation of episcopal areas and area synods, the creation of new Suffragan sees and the permanent delegation of episcopal functions by a diocesan bishop to a suffragan. It reports on these proposals to the diocesan synod of the diocese

concerned and to the General Synod. It also has an advisory rôle on matters affecting diocesan structure and is available for consultation by any diocesan bishop or synod.

(7) *The Doctrine Commission* exists to consider and advise the House of Bishops upon doctrinal matters referred to it by that House. It also has the function of making suggestions to that House as to what in its judgment are doctrinal issues of concern to the Church of England.

(8) *The Liturgical Commission* became a permanent Commission of the General Synod in 1971. Its functions include the preparation of forms of service for use in the Church of England and the exchange of information and advice on liturgical matters with other Churches.

THE CENTRAL COUNCILS AND THE DIOCESE
These Central Councils, most of which have their offices and headquarters in Church House, Westminster, must not be thought of as being aloof from the day to day work and problems of the local diocese. Their function is largely one of co-ordination, formulation of policy and the collection and dissemination of information and advice. In most cases there is very close liaison between the Central Councils and the dioceses. Most dioceses have their local Diocesan Committees corresponding to the Central Councils so that traffic to and from the centre and the locality is frequent. This can be illustrated from the following table

Central Committees	*Local diocesan counterpart* (The titles may vary)
Advisory Council for the Church's Ministry	Diocesan Advisory Council for Ministry
Board of Education	Diocesan Education Committee
Board for Mission and Unity	Diocesan Council for Mission and Unity
Board for Social Responsibility	Diocesan Council for Social Responsibility
Central Board of Finance	Diocesan Board of Finance
Council for the Care of Churches	Advisory Committee for the Care of Churches
The Liturgical Commission	Liturgical Advisory Committee
Central Readers Conference	Diocesan Association of Readers

XIII
The Church's Revenue and Expenditure

There are two common misunderstandings about the financial system of the Church of England. The first is the supposition that the Church is an extremely wealthy corporation and the second is the belief that it receives large sums of money from the State. Both are wholly without foundation. The Church is far from being wealthy and it depends for a vast amount of its resources on voluntary financial support. With regard to the second misunderstanding, the only money received from the State is that which is paid, by way of salaries, to Chaplains to the Forces, to Chaplains to HM Prisons, and to Hospital Chaplains, together with just less than £1 million (at present) to the Redundant Churches Fund and a further £4 million (at present) towards the repair of historic churches still in use.

THE CHURCH COMMISSIONERS FOR ENGLAND

The Church Commissioners came into existence in 1948, when Queen Anne's Bounty (1794) and the Ecclesiastical Commissioners (1836) were united. Prior to the breach with Rome the clergy were liable to pay to the Pope taxes based on the first year's profit of a benefice ('First Fruits') and a tenth part of the annual income ('Tenths'). When Henry VIII repudiated the Pope he annexed these payments, which henceforth were to go to the Crown. In 1704 Queen Anne restored these revenues to the Church to be administered by trustees known as the Governors of Queen Anne's Bounty. It is to be emphasised that this was not a grant by the State to the Church but the restoration to the Church of money which was annually paid by the clergy, and Queen Anne's expressed purpose in the Bounty was to use this money 'for the augmentation of the maintenance of the poor clergy'. By offering capital endowment grants from this small annual income — mainly in order to attract benefactions of at least equal amount — and with the further aid of some grants made by Parliament towards the endowment of new districts, the Governors of the Bounty were able by 1820 (when this form of augmentation practically ceased) to augment poor benefices by a capital sum of nearly £9 million. In addition, grants have been made to poor benefices to meet dilapidation payments on parsonage houses and for improvements and modernisation of the houses. For a time, after the Tithe Act of 1925, Queen Anne's Bounty was made responsible for the collection and distribution of benefice tithe.

In the early part of the nineteenth century the nation became conscious of the many abuses and inconsistencies in the administration of the Church of England, particularly with regard to the gross and glaring inequalities of wealth and property. Small benefices had large incomes, the wealth of episcopal estates and cathedral establishments was very considerable, while many of the large parishes had pathetically meagre endowments. There was much pluralism and non-residence. Moreover, the Industrial Revolution was changing the face of England, bringing with it the growth of vast new towns and a shift of population. No machinery existed whereby the Church could adjust itself and exercise adequately its ministry among the ever-growing industrial population.

In 1832 and in 1835 two Royal Commissions were appointed to inquire into the state of the Church in England and Wales and to recommend reforms. After the 1835 Commission had reported, an Act was passed in 1836 under which a permanent body was set up, called the Ecclesiastical Commissioners for England, whose task it became to carry out a great scheme of rearrangement of dioceses, to re-apportion bishops' incomes, and to re-model cathedral establishments. The large funds and properties which, as a result of these reforms, were diverted to the Commissioners were to be used to make additional provision for the cure of souls where most required. This came to include the augmentation of the incomes of poor benefices, and the provision of parsonage houses and stipends for assistant curates. The Commissioners did their work most efficiently and in the years which followed their creation they had laid upon them additional responsibilities, so that their office became a clearing house for most of the administrative problems of the Church, and particularly those concerned with 'the cure of souls'. In 1948 the Ecclesiastical Commissioners were dissolved and a new body was established under the title of *The Church Commissioners*. To this new body was transferred the work of both Queen Anne's Bounty and of the former Ecclesiastical Commissioners.

The Church Commissioners are a large body representative of both Church and State. They include the two archbishops and all the diocesan bishops; five deans or provosts; ten clergymen and ten laymen appointed by the General Synod; four laymen appointed by the Crown; four persons appointed by the Archbishop of Canterbury and some fifteen Officers of State and representatives of the Cities of London and York and of the Universities of Oxford and Cambridge; and the three Church Estates Commissioners. The Commissioners meet once a year. The Executive body is the Board of Governors which consists of the two archbishops, the three Church Estates Commissioners, and 23 members appointed by the Commissioners. It meets nine or ten times a year.

The three Church Estates Commissioners were created by an Act of 1850. The First and Third Commissioners are appointed respectively by the Crown and the Archbishop of Canterbury. These are both, strictly speaking, part-time appointments whose holders receive a salary and devote their time to the management and control of the day to day business of the Commissioners. The

Second Commissioner is unpaid and is a Member of Parliament who answers for the Commissioners in the House of Commons. Thus any action or failure of action on the part of the Commissioners can be questioned at any time in Parliament. In any case, the Commissioners are required to report annually to Parliament. Under an informal arrangement it has usually been the practice for the Second Commissioner to present Measures of the General Synod to the House of Commons.

The work of the Church Commissioners is very varied, but for convenience it may be divided as follows:

(1) *The management of the historic assets of the Church* entrusted to the Commissioners. The Commissioners own a considerable amount of agricultural, urban and commercial property. Some of their estates are ancient ecclesiastical endowments — land which has been Church property ever since it was donated to the Church centuries ago. Other estates were bought later as investments, using the proceeds of the sale of other investments. Their possession involves careful oversight and management, approval of new plans and works, improvements, sales and purchases, the collection of rents and the fostering of good relationships with the tenants. The Commissioners also hold a large and diverse Stock Exchange portfolio which is managed to secure good income growth for present and future generations.

(2) *Support of the clergy.* The primary call on the Commissioners' income is the payment of clergy stipends. They have also been appointed by the General Synod as the Church's *Central Stipends Authority.* In 1984 the Commissioners provided just under half the money for the stipends of the clergy and each year they try to make more money available for this purpose, which is distributed among the dioceses on a selective basis according to perceived needs. As the Central Stipends Authority the Commissioners keep under review and adjust the stipends of dignitaries, and consult diocesan authorities and advise them on levels of the pay of clergymen, deaconesses and licensed lay workers. They make grants towards the stipends of full-time chaplains at universities, polytechnics and Church of England Colleges of Education, they make capital grants of up to 50 per cent to meet gifts or bequests for the capital accounts of diocesan stipend funds and the provision of suitable parsonage houses, and they may, from time to time, make capital available for new parsonage houses. They may also assist by allocating funds for providing churches, church halls and houses of the clergy in new housing areas. An increasing call on the Commissioners' money is the payment of

the pensions of the clergy and their widows, for which they provide virtually all the necessary finance. The detailed arrangements for individual payments are made in conjunction with the Church of England Pensions Board (see p.61). The Commissioners also provide loans to the Pensions Board to assist the clergy and their widows with retirement housing.

(3) *Administration.* Under the Pastoral Measure 1983 the Commissioners are responsible for dealing with proposals for pastoral reorganisation initiated by diocesan authorities. They have the further duty under the Measure of deciding whether churches which have been declared redundant should be made available for suitable other uses, be preserved, or be demolished. The Commissioners are also responsible for considering all proposals for the provision and sale of parsonage houses and certain transactions affecting diocesan glebe.

VOLUNTARY OFFERINGS

It is clear that, although the Church Commissioners do a very great deal to maintain the financial stability of the Church of England, there is still a wide field uncovered by their efforts. Voluntary contributions have to cover such large items as the portion of clergy stipends not covered by the Commissioners grants, the training of men and women for ordained and lay ministry, the mission of the Church at home and abroad, the upkeep of the fabric of churches and cathedrals, together with their running expenses, and the financial provision for the efficient administration of the parishes, the dioceses and the Church of England as a whole.

Income and expenditure can be regarded as being on three levels — the parochial, the diocesan and the central — the link between them being the quota system. In each diocese every parish is carefully assessed for a contribution to the diocese (the parochial quota); each diocese is assessed for a contribution to central funds (the diocesan quota). The quota represents not an imposition or a levy but the share which the parish or diocese pays towards the work of the whole Church of which the parish or the diocese is itself an essential part.

(1) *Parochial.* The expenses at parochial level include the payment of salaries of church officials such as the organist, verger, cleaner, etc., the working expenses of the incumbent, the upkeep of the fabric of the church building and its heating, lighting and insurance, the maintenance of the churchyard, contributions to the Church overseas and charitable bodies, the running expenses of the parish and the parochial quota to the diocese, a large part of which, in practice, is used to

contribute to the salaries of the parochial clergy, deaconesses and lay workers. Income comes almost entirely from weekly offerings, covenanted subscriptions and church collections. Christian stewardship has greatly augmented the income of many parishes. The majority of parishes, either regularly or occasionally, receive aid from diocesan funds, either directly to meet urgent repairs to the church building or for new churches and church halls, and more indirectly through the augmentation of the stipends of the clergy, deaconesses and lay workers.

(2) *Diocesan.* In addition to the expenditure just outlined, each diocese requires specialist workers — e.g. a Director of Education, a Diocesan Secretary and Surveyor, secretaries and officers of Boards and Councils, etc. There is the cost of in-service training for the clergy, the provision of lay training, grants to the families of those who are training for the ordained ministry of the Church and the repair of parsonage houses. Then there is the cost of administration and the diocesan quota to central funds. The income at diocesan level comes almost entirely through the parochial quota, supplemented in some cases by annual subscriptions from individuals and corporate bodies and by a certain limited number of legacies.

(3) *Central.* The Church's central funds (other than those administered by the Church Commissioners) are administered by the Central Board of Finance (see p.60). Each diocese has a representative on the Central Board, the income of which is derived from the diocesan quota. The charges on central funds are mainly payments to the Central Boards and Councils of the General Synod, payments towards the training of men and women for ministry, and grants on behalf of the Church of England to Anglican and Ecumenical bodies. To give an indication of its level of expenditure, in 1984 the Central Board asked the dioceses to contribute over £3 million towards the cost of training for ministry and over £2½ million towards the cost of its other activities.

XIV
The Church's Legal System

A. ECCLESIASTICAL LAW

History

From the earliest times it has been conceded that a Church has the right to make its own laws for its members. Every society has its rules for the management of its own affairs, and the members of a particular society agree to abide by the rules of that society. In the case of the Church, however, there is a higher sanction for the formulation and enforcement of rules and regulations for its members. That sanction rests upon the commission given by Jesus Christ to his apostles: 'What things soever ye shall bind on earth shall be bound in heaven; and what things soever ye shall loose on earth shall be loosed in heaven' (Matt. 18.18). The commission to 'bind' and to 'loose' means to 'declare forbidden' and to 'declare allowed'. The first apostles regarded rules and regulations as of considerable importance, and one has only to refer to St Paul's detailed rules for divine worship in the Church at Corinth (I Corinthians) or to the regulations made at the first Council of Jerusalem (Acts 15) concerning the admission of Gentiles into the Christian Church to see how necessary it was at a very early stage that corporate legislation needed to be promulgated. And so in every generation the Church, by virtue of Christ's commission, has made whatever rules have been necessary for the ordering of its corporate life. Now the Church is not a body of perfected saints but is made up of ordinary frail human beings. It follows, therefore, that unless chaos is to prevail the rules and regulations which it makes must be more than exhortations which anyone can set aside when he wishes. Instead, they must be laws which can be enforced and to which are attached penalties for their non-observance.

As the Church grew and developed so did the need for regulations. The name given to such laws and enactments was *canon*. It is derived from the Greek word *kanon*, meaning a straight rod or line by which to measure things; hence, a rule or law by which actions can be judged. In the early days canons were local laws based on local custom and local episcopal regulation. Later, local Councils and then General Councils passed canons of more or less universal application. With the growth of the Papacy the decretals of Popes received an ever-growing importance. The next stage was the collection, arrangement, and codification of these diverse and scattered pronouncements.

England, like the rest of the Western Church, came under the authority of this ever-growing Canon Law, and the collections of Church laws that were employed by the rest of the Church were of authority in this country. In addition, England had its own local compilations and there was also some Statute Law governing certain aspects of Church life and administration. A change came, however, with the Reformation, the immediate aim of which was to terminate the Papal authority in this country and to assert that the King was the supreme head on earth of the Church of England. Upon the Canon Law of the Church the Reformation had a two-fold effect. The first was retrospective, in that under the Act of Submission of the Clergy in 1533 it was ordered that of the canons up to then in force only those should be acknowledged which were not contrary to the laws of the realm or derogatory to the King's prerogative. The second effect looked forward, in that under the same Act changes in the Church's law could be made only by or with the express or implied consent of the secular power. Thus, from the time of the Reformation laws for the Church could be made only in one of two ways. The first was by Parliament (Statute Law) and the second was through the promulgation of canons by Convocation, provided that the Royal Licence to make canons had been secured and that the Royal Assent to such canons was given. No canons should be repugnant to the Royal prerogative or contrary to the Statute Law. Various attempts at legislation along the latter lines were made by Convocation in the sixteenth century, but it was not until the reign of James I that a body of canons (known as 'The Canons of 1603') was passed by Convocation and received the Royal Assent. The majority of these canons represented a codification of the series of Royal Injunctions, Articles and orders which had been put out during the reign of Elizabeth as supplements to the Statute Law. This body of canons remained regulative for the Church until 1945, when a process of radical revision was initiated and which ended in 1969. In addition a considerable amount of ecclesiastical legislation has been passed by Statute in Parliament, and in 1919 there came into existence the new system of legislation by Measures of the Church Assembly and, after 1969, of the General Synod (see p.51).

THE PRESENT POSITION

The Law of the Church of England is at present drawn from the following sources:

(1) *Statute Law,* in the form of Acts of Parliament and — more recently — Measures of the Church Assembly and the General Synod, which have the force of Acts of Parliament.

(2) *Subordinate legislation,* such as Orders in Council and Statutory Rules and Orders, made under the authority of an Act or a Measure.

(3) *Common Law*, which is that part of the law concerning the Church which is based on custom and immemorial practice, either prior to the Reformation or since.

(4) *The Canons of 1969*, and canons made subsequently by the General Synod.

(5) That *part of the Pre-Reformation Canon Law* which was in operation in England prior to 1533 and which at that date was 'not contrariant or repugnant to the laws, statutes and customs of this realm, nor to the damage and hurt of the King's prerogative royal', and which has not been subsequently repealed or amended. Two points are to be noted. In the first place, this pre-Reformation law was retained not because it was the work of the Papacy but because it had been long observed in England and had thus acquired the legal status of Custom, or Common Law. In the second place, much of this pre-Reformation Canon Law which was retained after 1533 has subsequently been the subject of parliamentary Statutes and has been embodied in legal forms more suited to the life of this country. What is left, however, is still part of the ecclesiastical law, with one important proviso — that such canons have 'been continued and uniformly recognised and acted upon in England since the Reformation'.

A matter of some ambiguity is the precise extent of the authority of the ecclesiastical law. The position may be summarised as follows.

(1) That part of the ecclesiastical law which is embodied in Acts of Parliament and in Measures of the Church Assembly, and the General Synod, is binding upon both the clergy and the laity.

(2) Such pre-Reformation canons and ancient usage which remain lawful are binding upon both the clergy and the laity.

(3) The Canons of 1969 are not legally binding on the laity (other than certain lay officers), except in so far as they declare the ancient usage and law of the Church of England allowed in 1533.

B. THE CHURCH COURTS
History
Every legal system presupposes the existence of Courts to enforce the laws when breaches of them occur. It is not otherwise with the ecclesiastical law. Some of the latter is enforceable in the secular Courts, but in addition the Church has its own Courts.

It is unnecessary to give much space to the history of Church Courts in England. In the Middle Ages there gradually grew up a network of Church Courts, whose jurisdiction covered a very wide field, embracing the laity as well as the clergy. Church worship, doctrine and property, marriages, wills, legitimacy, probate, oaths, and personal behaviour and morals (e.g. adultery, sabbath breaking, drunkenness), were among the variety of matters which fell within their cognizance. Final appeal lay to the Pope, although such appeals were normally heard in England before a Papal delegate. The Reformation made surprisingly little change in the system and jurisdiction of the Courts, the most important being the substitution of the King in Chancery for the Pope as the final court of appeal. Nevertheless, the history of the Church Courts in this country during the last 300 years has been a long story of a gradual loss of jurisdiction. Divorce and matrimonial causes and testamentary jurisdiction have been transferred to secular Courts, and a number of offences are now triable by the Criminal Courts. The abolition of Church rates and tithe has further reduced their business, while most of their jurisdiction over the morals of the laity has become obsolete. The result is that today the Ecclesiastical Courts 'are concerned with the discipline of the clergy and of laymen holding office in the Church, questions of doctrine and ritual, protecting Church property, and civil disputes relating to ecclesiastical matters'. (Peter Archer, *The Queen's Courts* (1956) p.204).

It will be apparent that, although their jurisdiction has been severely curtailed, the ancient Church Courts still remain as the apparatus for enforcing a great part of the ecclesiastical law. They form a three-tiered system. First there is the Consistory Court of the Diocese, secondly there are the Courts of the Province, and thirdly there are the courts of appeal.

DIOCESAN COURTS

Each bishop has a diocesan court for administering ecclesiastical law within his diocese. In the Diocese of Canterbury this Court is known as the *Commissary Court,* but in all other English dioceses it is called the *Consistory Court.* The judge of the Court in the Diocese of Canterbury has the title of *Commissary-General;* elsewhere he is called the *Chancellor.* In effect, the judge *is* the bishop acting in a judicial capacity and his judgments are the bishop's judgments. Therefore, no appeal lies from him to the bishop. He must be a barrister of seven years' standing or a person who has held high judicial office. He usually acts as standing counsel to the bishop and the diocesan authorities and gives advice on matters of legal difficulty. A word may be added about the other diocesan legal officer — the *Registrar.* As the chief officer of the Consistory Court he keep the records of the Court and prepares faculties; as an officer of the bishop he keeps a record of the bishop's public acts (the Bishop's Register) and is his adviser on legal matters. He is a solicitor.

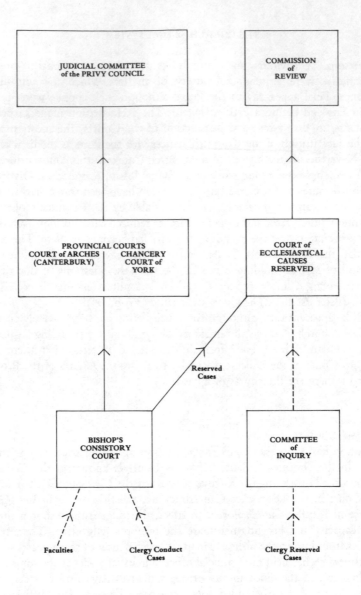

THE CHURCH COURTS

- - - ▷ - - - Introduction of Cases

———▷——— Course of Appeal

The principal jurisdiction of the Consistory Court lies in the granting of faculties for the alteration of church fabric and furniture (see p.34); here the Chancellor sits alone. It is before this Court, also, that a clergyman may be prosecuted, if his offence does not involve a matter of doctrine, ritual, or ceremonial. Conduct unbecoming the office and work of a clerk in Holy Orders, and serious, persistent or continuous neglect of duty are examples of ecclesiastical offences which are triable before this Court. At the hearing the Chancellor (or Commissary-General) sits as judge, with four assessors (two clerical and two lay) to act as jury. Appeal against judgment in any Consistory Court, not involving matters of doctrine, ritual or ceremonial ('Reserved Cases'), may be lodged in the Provincial Court. A further, and final, appeal lies to the Judicial Committee of the Privy Council.

PROVINCIAL COURTS

In the Province of Canterbury the provincial Court is known as the *Court of Arches* and is presided over by the *Dean of the Court of Arches*. The origin of this title is of interest. From the twelfth century onwards the church of St Mary of the Arches (St Mary-le-Bow), together with 12 other churches in the City of London, formed a 'peculiar' (see p.14) of the Archbishop of Canterbury. This peculiar had its own Court, whose judge was called a Dean and who took his title (Dean of the Arches) from the name of the church (St Mary of the Arches) where the Court sat. Moreover, because this was a peculiar of the archbishop, it was convenient that the Court of the Province of Canterbury should sit in the same building. From the beginning of the sixteenth century the same person was appointed judge of both Courts. In this way the judge of the provincial Court acquired the title of the less important office, the Dean of the Court of Arches. In the Province of York the provincial Court is known as the *Chancery Court of York,* and its judge bears the title of *Auditor.* Under an Act of 1874 the same person must be appointed judge of both provincial Courts. There are four other judges in each Court, two appointed by the prolocutor of the Lower House of Convocation of the relevant province and two, being communicant laymen possessing judicial experience, appointed by the Chairman of the House of Laity of the General Synod after consultation with the Lord Chancellor. Each provincial Court is the court of appeal from the Consistory Courts within the province in faculty cases not involving matters of doctrine, ritual or ceremonial, and also in proceedings against priests and deacons for offences not involving such matters. In the former cases the Dean of the Arches or Auditor sits alone; in proceedings against priests and deacons all five judges sit.

The Archbishop of Canterbury (but not of York) has a *Court of Faculties,* presided over by the *Master of the Faculties* who is always the Dean of the Arches (see p.73). This Court deals with matters connected with the powers transferred at the Reformation from the Pope to the Archbishop, in his capacity as Primate of All England. It grants *special* marriage licences (see p.28), it appoints and removes public notaries (officials entitled to prepare and certify certain classes of legal documents), and grants faculties in matters which are the specific concern of the Primate.

COURT OF ECCLESIASTICAL CAUSES RESERVED

It will have been noted that matters involving doctrine, ritual or ceremonial do not fall within the jurisdiction of the diocesan and provincial Courts. The Court of Ecclesiastical Causes Reserved is a court of first instance for proceedings against the clergy for offences involving such matters. Before a case is brought before the Court the bishop of the diocese in which the accused clergyman works must refer the matter to a specially constituted committee of enquiry, consisting of one member of the Upper House and two members of the Lower House of the Convocation of the province and two chancellors of dioceses in the province. If the committee recommends further proceedings the case is brought before the Court of Ecclesiastical Causes Reserved. The Court is also the court of appeal from Consistory Courts in faculty cases which involve doctrine, ritual or ceremonial. The Court consists of five judges appointed by the Crown, two of whom are persons who hold or have held high judicial office and who are communicants, and the other three are diocesan bishops or former diocesan bishops. The final appeal from this Court is to a *Commission of Review,* consisting of three lay Lords of Appeal who are communicants, and two diocesan bishops who are members of the House of Lords.

The reason why cases involving doctrine, ritual and ceremonial are dealt with in a manner different from other cases is because in the past it was thought that the Judicial Committee of the Privy Council, which was the final court of appeal in all cases, made decisions in these particular matters on an inadequate understanding by secular judges of the history and development of doctrine, ritual and ceremonial. To many it was intolerable that the final voice in deciding questions of the Church's doctrine and worship should be that, not of the Church, but of a Court of laymen set up by the State and whose judgments were binding upon the lower courts which were admittedly spiritual courts.

For the trial of bishops there is a different procedure from the trial of other clergymen.

XV
The Anglican Communion and the Ecumenical Movement

THE ANGLICAN COMMUNION

The Christian religion is fundamentally a missionary religion. 'Go ye and make disciples of all the nations'; 'Ye shall be my witnesses both in Jerusalem, and in all Judea and Samaria, and unto the uttermost parts of the earth'. These are the instructions which the Christian Church received from Jesus Christ and it has been in fulfilment of these that the Church has spread from Jerusalem to east and west, across Europe and to England, and beyond. As the Church became settled in each new area so it sent missionaries to other places. From England, Wilfred, Willibrord, and Boniface went to Germany in the seventh and eighth centuries, and others went to Scandinavia. Unfortunately, for many centuries the stream of missionary enterprise in England dried up and there was little or no effort to extend the Christian faith beyond these shores, but after the Reformation and the English secession from Rome the stream started to flow anew. That it did so was closely connected with the expansion of British secular influence abroad. In the seventeenth and eighteenth centuries the Church's mission overseas rapidly increased because of the creation of the Missionary Societies and voluntary societies within the Church which raised the funds, provided the missionaries, and for long had the general oversight and responsibility for the work in their areas. The Society for Promoting Christian Knowledge (SPCK) was founded in 1698/9 by clergy and laity and one of its main objects was to consult on the best means and methods of 'promoting Religion and learning in any part of His Majesty's Plantations abroad'. Three years later (1701) Thomas Bray founded the Society for the Propagation of the Gospel in Foreign Parts (SPG) for the purpose of sending out 'Church of England clergy to the colonies, to instruct the colonists in the Christian religion, and to preach the Gospel amongst the heathen'. In 1799 the Church Missionary Society was founded (originally called the Society of Mission to Africa and the East), and in the nineteenth century the extension of the Anglican Church into all parts of the world continued apace.

As the Church of England spread and as local communities of Christians began to appear, the need for territorial organisation began to be felt and the Church overseas began to be divided into dioceses and provinces. In the beginning these dioceses were dependent almost entirely upon this country for men, money and policy. Today, they are independent and provinces are autonomous. When the region is too large or diverse for an effective province, there have been created constitutional Councils with stated limited powers. There are some 417 dioceses of the Anglican Communion and its member Churches, Provinces and Councils are as follows:

The Anglican Church of Australia
The Episcopal Church of Brazil

The Church of the Province of Burma
The Church of the Province of Burundi, Rwanda and Zaire
The Anglican Church of Canada
The Church of the Province of Central Africa
The Church of Ceylon
The Holy Catholic Church in China (Chung Hua Shong Kung Hui)
The Council of the Church of East Asia
The Church of England
The Church of the Province of the Indian Ocean
The Church of Ireland
The Holy Catholic Church in Japan (Nippon Sei Ko Kai)
The Episcopal Church in Jerusalem and the Middle East
The Church of the Province of Kenya
The Church of the Province of Melanesia
The Church of the Province of New Zealand
The Church of the Province of Nigeria
The Anglican Church of Papua New Guinea
The Scottish Episcopal Church
The Church of the Province of South Africa
The Anglican Church of the Southern Cone of America
The South Pacific Anglican Council
The Church in the Province of the Sudan
The Church of the Province of Tanzania
The Church of Uganda
The Episcopal Church of the United States of America (ECUSA)
The Church in Wales
The Church of the Province of West Africa
The Church in the Province of the West Indies

In India, Pakistan and Bangladesh the former Anglican dioceses are now parts of new independent united Churches.

The Anglican Communion has been defined as 'a world-wide family of Churches and dioceses which

(1)   trace their origins to the post-Reformation expansion of the Church of England in association with the other episcopalian or Anglican Churches of the British Isles;

(2)   are in communion with the See of Canterbury and freely recognize the Archbishop of Canterbury as the Principal Archbishop and the focus of unity within the Communion;

(3)   Uphold and propagate the catholic and apostolic faith based on the scriptures interpreted in the light of Christian tradition, scholarship and reason, a process which has found its typical Anglican expression in the Prayer Books and Ordinals of the sixteenth and seventeenth centuries or their derivatives throughout the Anglican Communion, and in successive versions of the "Lambeth quadrilateral", which was first set out in the Lambeth Conference of 1888.'

The growth in the number of autonomous provinces and councils has not resulted in the disintegration of the Anglican Communion because of four factors which preserve its unity.

(1)   *The Archbishop of Canterbury.* As the Anglican Church has developed into an international communion a position of seniority has continued to be ascribed to the see of Canterbury, but this seniority is understood as a ministry of service and support to the other Anglican Churches, not as a form of domination over them. The Archbishop of Canterbury has great spiritual and moral authority throughout the Anglican Communion, he is constantly asked for advice and counsel by overseas bishops and he is President of the Lambeth Conference, but he makes no claim to a primacy of universal jurisdiction.

(2)   *The Lambeth Conference.* The first Lambeth Conference was held in 1867, at the request of the bishops of Canada and the United States. It was held at Lambeth Palace and 76 bishops, out of the 144 summoned, attended. Since that date a further ten Conferences have been held and at the 1978 Conference 459 bishops attended, which is an indication of the growth of the Communion in 110 years. The Lambeth Conference has no legislative or executive powers; it is a purely deliberative body, meeting in private. Its decisions are recorded in a series of resolutions, but these resolutions are expressions of opinion and are not legislative decisions, although they must necessarily carry great moral and spiritual weight.

(3)   *The Anglican Consultative Council,* which was established in 1969 and which includes clergy and laity representative of the Churches of the Anglican Communion. Its task is to share information, advise on provincial structures, develop policies for the world mission of the Church and to advise Anglican Churches on matters arising out of union negotiations. It meets every two or three years. It has a full-time Secretary-General who travels widely among the Churches of the Anglican Communion.

(4)   *Meetings of Primates of the Anglican Communion* for regular consultation. This followed a request made by the Lambeth Conference in 1978 and three meetings have been held since that date.

In 1973 the Anglican Consultative Council launched *Partners In Mission* (PIM), the object of which was 'to develop and foster more effective patterns of consultation and working relationships between the member Churches of the Anglican Communion'. Broadly speaking, the pattern of Partners in Mission is that, first, each Church shall examine, with the help of chosen partners, its priorities, plans and resources. The partners are a small group of people representative of the other Churches in the Anglican Communion, together with some non-Anglicans, and whilst the process is proceeding the partners are consulted about what their own contribution to the mission in that place might be.

Partners in Mission must not be confused with the *Partnership for World Mission.*, inaugurated in 1978, which is a co-ordinating body bringing together representatives of the General Synod, of the eight 'recognised' missionary societies and of the Church Army and the Mothers' Union, together with 16 other agencies as associate members. The object of this Partnership is to establish better co-ordination between the societies themselves and between them and the official Church as represented by the General Synod, without at the same time squandering the vision, the enthusiasm and the fellowship engendered by the voluntary societies. The Partnership is a forum for co-ordination and joint planning, a source of advice to the Church of England on world mission and evangelism, and a body to stimulate prayer and concern for world mission throughout the Church.

THE ECUMENICAL MOVEMENT

The Church of England has played a major part in that 'coming together' of the Christian Churches which is known as the Ecumenical Movement. The word 'ecumenical' comes from a Greek word meaning 'the whole inhabited globe', and the movement represents the world-wide drawing together of the Churches. After the Reformation in the sixteenth century it looked for two or three hundred years as if the Christian Church was to be perpetually divided into smaller and smaller fragments, but in the last hundred years the tide has turned and Churches have been learning to think together, to pray together and to work together. In 1910 a great World Missionary Conference was held at Edinburgh and from this event almost all the modern movements for Christian co-operation and unity are derived. The tide flowed in three channels. The first was that of missionary co-operation — leading in 1921 to the foundation of the International Missionary Council, containing representatives of most Churches engaged in overseas work. The second was that of thinking out together the meaning of the Christian faith which the Churches held in common and the reasons for the divisions between them — what was called the

Faith and Order Movement. The third channel of co-operation was in the direction of what may be called practical Christianity — the living of the Christian life in the modern world. This was known as the Life and Work Movement. These last two channels — that of Faith and Order and that of Life and Work — flowed together into the plan for a *World Council of Churches,* which was formally constituted at Amsterdam in 1948. The International Missionary Council, although very closely related to the work of the World Council of Churches, retained its separate identity until 1961, when it was integrated with the WCC as the Commission on World Mission and Evangelism.

The basis of the WCC, as set out in 1961, is in these terms:— 'The World Council of Churches is a fellowship of Churches which confess the Lord Jesus Christ as God and Saviour according to the Scriptures, and therefore seek to fulfil together their common calling to the glory of the one God, Father, Son and Holy Spirit'. The aims of the Council are to call the Churches to the goal of visible unity, to facilitate the common witness of the Church, to support the Churches in their world-wide missionary and evangelistic task, to express the common concern of the Churches in the service of human need and the breaking down of barriers between people, and to carry on the work of the world movements for Faith and Order, Life and Work, and that of the International Missionary Council. The Headquarters of the WCC are in Geneva and it has some three hundred member churches, including thirty which are associated. Almost every province of the Anglican Communion is included, together with the Orthodox Churches and all the main Reformed traditions. The Church of Rome is not a member, but sends official observers to all main World Council meetings. The General Synod Board for Mission and Unity is responsible for matters relating to the participation of the Church of England in the WCC.

The member Churches relate to the Council's organisation in two ways. First, through the representative structure of the Assembly, which meets every seven or eight years, and the Central Committee, elected by the Assembly and meeting annually. Secondly, through the Programme Units and sub-units. The bulk of the Council's work is conducted in the Programme Units of which there are three:

(1) *Faith and Witness* This deals with Faith and Order, world mission and evangelism, and the Church and Society. It includes the Commission on World Mission and Evangelism, and other sub-units of the Programme are concerned with dialogue with living faiths and ideologies and with theological education.

(2) *Justice and Service* This represents the WCC's concern with international affairs and the developing countries. It includes the Commission on Inter-Church Aid,

Refugee and World Service, and also the Programme to Combat Racism. The latter was established in 1969 in order to discover ways of helping the Churches to reconsider their involvement in racially discriminatory attitudes. A feature of the Programme is the Special Fund which was set up to make grants to organisations of the racially oppressed who were working effectively against their oppressors. This Fund is entirely separate from the WCC General Fund, to which member Churches contribute, and it obtains its income solely from specially earmarked contributions from Churches, from governments and from numerous private gifts.

(3) *Education and Renewal* This Unit has a three-fold purpose. First, it is concerned with ways in which Christian congregations can be assisted in their task of witness, worship and spirituality. Secondly, it is involved in the development of new educational methods, and in particular those related to the use of the Bible in Christian teaching. Thirdly, it is concerned with the place of women, young people and children in the life of the Church and Society.

The WCC provides through the *Ecumenical Press Service* a regular news service to the world's press, to TV and to radio, and its two periodicals, *One World* and *Ecumenical Review* are in circulation in this country.

There are seven Regional Conferences recognised by the WCC and they include the *Conference of European Churches,* of which the Church of England is a member. It was officially constituted in 1964 and has a membership of 117 Churches from almost all European countries. It is an important meeting place for Orthodox, Old Catholic and Protestant Churches, and although it is not a member, the Roman Catholic Church is represented by a strong group of observers. It is one of the few ways in which Churches from East and West Europe can meet.

The British Council of Churches was inaugurated in 1942 and is a fellowship of Christians in the British Isles 'which confess the Lord Jesus as God and Saviour according to the Scriptures and therefore seeks to fulfil together their common calling to the glory of the one God, Father, Son and Holy Spirit'. The majority of Churches in the British Isles are represented on the BCC, with the exception of the Roman Catholic Church, which, however, appoints official consultant/observers. Of the Church of England representatives ten are elected by the General Synod, seven are appointed by the Standing Committee of the General Synod and seven are appointed by the two Archbishops. The Council possesses departments for Community Affairs, Ecumenical Affairs, and International Affairs. Christian Aid is a Division of the BCC and is charged with organising the joint response of the British Churches to the needs of refugees and victims of disaster throughout the world and is concerned also with community and economic developments in the less developed parts of the world. Another Division of the BCC is the Conference for World Mission, founded in 1912 as the Conference of Missionary Societies in Great Britain and Ireland. It is affiliated to the Commission on World Mission and Evangelism of the WCC and its object is to be a centre of co-operative consultation, planning and common action among missionary agencies in Britain. It is the recognised channel of the relationships between the missionary enterprise as a whole and government departments. The BCC sponsors the annual Week of Prayer for Christian Unity which is held from 18th to 25th January. Local Councils of Churches have been established in many areas and there are over 700 of these which are in association with the BCC.

The Anglican Centre in Rome was established in 1966 following the historic visit of the Archbishop of Canterbury (Dr Michael Ramsey) to Rome. The Centre is a channel for the extension of relationships between the Anglican Church and the Church of Rome and is a meeting place for members of the Anglican Communion and other Churches, particularly the Roman Catholic Church, for discussion and prayer. It possesses a library of Anglican history, theology, and liturgy, thus providing working facilities for students and scholars of all Christian denominations. It provides a focal point for Anglican collaboration with the various agencies of the Roman Catholic Church and in particular its Secretariat for Promoting Christian Unity.

Index

Advisory Committee for the Care of Churches, 34, 61
Advowson, 21
Alternative Service Book, 29, 30
Anglican Centre in Rome, 81
Anglican Communion, The, 52, 75ff; Secretary-General of, 47, 59, 77
Anglican Consultative Council, 52, 59, 77
Appropriation, 16
Archbishop, 5ff, 22, 54f, 64, 73f; see also Canterbury, Archbishop of;
    York, Archbishop of,
Archdeaconry, Archdeacon, 12f, 23, 34, 36, 46, 54, 56
Arches, Court of, 73; Dean of, 56, 73
Archpriest, 13
Area Bishop, 11
Assistant Bishop, 11f

Banns of Marriage, 28
Benefice, 15f
Bishop, 7ff, 21ff, 25, 37, 54, 64, 71; appointment of, 46f; in House of Lords, 48;
    Suffragan, 11, 46, 54; Assistant, 11f; Area, 11
Bishop's Council, 46, 53
British Council of Churches, 52, 59, 80f
Burial in Churchyard, Right of, 29

Canon, Residentiary, 39; Non-Residentiary (Honorary), 39
Canons, Canon Law, 49, 50, 68ff
Canterbury, Province of, 5f, 8, 73; Archbishop of, 5f, 46, 56, 74, 77
Care of Churches, Council for, 61; Advisory Committee for, 34
Cathedral, 37ff
Cathedral Advisory Commission for England, 61
Central Readers' Conference, 57
Central Stipends Authority, 24, 65
Chancellor, Cathedral, 38; diocesan, 34, 71
Chancery Court of York, 73
Chaplain, parish, 16, 42; Armed Forces, 42; prison, 42; hospital, 42f;
    college, university, polytechnic, school, 43; industrial, 43
Chapter, cathedral, 6, 37f, 40, 47; deanery, 13f
Church Army Evangelist, 26
Church Assembly, The, 50
Church Commissioners, The, 18, 24, 29, 63ff
Churchwarden, 22, 24, 32, 34ff
Collation, 23
Commissary-General, 71
Commission of Review, 74
Commissioners, Church, see Church Commissioners
Conference of European Churches, 52, 59, 80
Confirmation of Bishop's Election, 47
Consistory Court, 34, 71f
Conventional District, 17
Convocation, 50, 52, 54

Courts, Church, 70ff; of Arches, 73; Chancery Court of York, 73;
    Consistory, 34, 71f; of Ecclesiastical Causes Reserved, 74; of Faculties, 74;
    Commission of Review, 74
Covenant, Local, 20
Crown Appointments, 21, 46f, 48
Curate, 24f

Deaconess, 25
Dean, of Cathedral, 37, 39f; Rural, 13f; of Christianity, 13; of Arches, 56, 73
Deanery Chapter, 13f
Deanery Synod, 14, 53f
Dignitary, 37
Diocesan Synod, 10, 53f
Diocese, 7ff, 18, 40f, 62, 67, 71
Dioceses Commission, 61
Doctrine Commission, 62

Ecclesiastical Causes Reserved, Court of, 74
Ecclesiastical Commissioners, The, 64
Ecclesiastical Law, 68ff
Ecumenical Movement, 78ff
Education, The General Synod Board of, 57f
Election of Bishop, 47
Electoral Roll, 28, 31, 32, 53
Enthronement of Bishop, 47
Establishment, Church, 45ff
Evangelist, Church Army, 26

Faculty, 34, 73
Faculties, Court of, 74; Master of, 74
Fees, Ecclesiastical, 24, 29
Finance, Central Board of, 60f, 67

General Synod, The, 50f, 54ff
Group Ministry, 18
Guardian of the Spiritualities, 6
Guild Churches, 20

Holy Matrimony, 27f
Homage by Bishops, 48
House of Lords, Bishops in, 48

Impropriation, 16
Incumbent, 15ff, 21ff, 27ff, 36, 51f; see Rector, Vicar
Induction, 23
Institution, 23

Laity, Layman, 27, 54, 55
Lambeth Conference, 77
Law, Ecclesiastical, *see* Ecclesiastical Law
Lecturer, 25
Licence, Marriage, 28; Special Marriage, 28
Liturgical Commission, 62
Local Ecumenical Project, 19f

Marriage in Church, 27f
Master of Faculties, 74
Measures of Church Assembly and General Synod, 49, 51; Benefice (Right of
    Presentation) Measure 1931, 21f; Church of England (Worship and Doctrine)
    Measure 1974, 29f, 33, 49, 52; Deacons (Ordination of Women) Measure, 25;
    Inspection of Churches Measure 1955, 12f, 33; Parsonage Measures 1938-47, 33;
    Pastoral Measure 1983, 17ff, 33, 66; Patronage (Benefice) Measure, 21, 22, 33;
    Prayer Book (Versions of the Bible) Measure 1965, 30
Metropolitan, 5
Ministry, Advisory Council for the Church's, 57
Minster, 15
Mission and Unity, Board for, 59
Missionary Societies, 75, 79
Monastic Orders, 14, 43ff

National Society, The, 58f
Non-Stipendiary Minister, 25

Organist, 33, 35

Parish, 15ff
Parishioners, Rights and Duties of, 27ff
Parish Clerk, 33, 36
Parish Worker, 26
Parochial Church Council, 22, 32ff
Parochial Church Meeting, 31, 53
Parson, 21
Partners in Mission, 78
Partnership for World Mission, 78
Pastoral Committee, 18
Pastoral Measure, 1983, 17ff
Patron, Patronage, 15, 21f
Peculiar, 14
Pensions Board, Church of England, 61, 66
Prebend, Prebendary, 39
Precentor, 38
Priest-in-Charge, 21
Primate, 5
Privy Council, Judicial Committee of the, 49, 73, 74
Prolocutor, 54
Province, 5f; *see* Canterbury, York

Provost, 40, 46, 56

Queen Anne's Bounty, 63

Rate, Church, 33
Reader, 26
Rector, 16; *see* Incumbent
Redundant Church, 18f, 66
Registrar, Diocesan, 71
Religious Orders, 14, 43ff
Rome, Anglican Centre in, 81
Rural Deanery, Rural Dean, *see* Deanery, Rural; Dean, Rural

Sacrist, 38
Sequestration, Sequestrator, 24, 35
Sexton, 33, 36
Sharing of Church Buildings Act 1969, 19
Six Preachers, The (Canterbury Cathedral), 40
Social Responsibility, Board for, 59f
Standing Committee of General Synod, 56; of Diocesan Synod, 53; of Parochial
    Church Council, 32
Succentor, 38
Suffragan Bishop, 11, 46, 54
Superintendent Registrar's Certificate, 28
Surrogate, 28
Synod, *see* General Synod, Diocesan Synod, Deanery Synod
Synodical Government, 50ff

Team Ministry, 17
Tithe, 15f
Translation of Bishop, 9
Treasurer, Cathedral, 38

Verger, 33, 35
Vicar, 16; *see* Incumbent
Vicar-General, 47

World Council of Churches, 52, 59, 79f
Worship and Doctrine Measure, 1974, 29f, 33, 49, 52

York, Province of, 5, 8, 50, 54, 73; Archbishop of, 5f, 46